Group's

Blockbuster

MOVIE ILLUSTRATIONS

The Sequel

Bryan Belknap

Group
Loveland, Colorado

Group's R.E.A.L. Guarantee to you:

This Group resource incorporates our R.E.A.L. approach to ministry—one that encourages long-term retention and life transformation. It's ministry that's:

Relational
Because learner-to-learner interaction enhances learning and builds Christian friendships.

Experiential
Because what learners experience through discussion and action sticks with them up to 9 times longer than what they simply hear or read.

Applicable
Because the aim of Christian education is to equip learners to be both hearers and doers of God's Word.

Learner-based
Because learners understand and retain more when the learning process takes into consideration how they learn best.

Group's BlockBuster Movie Illustrations: *The Sequel*

Copyright © 2003 Bryan Belknap

CREDITS

Editor: *Kelli B. Trujillo*
Creative Development Editor: *Amy Simpson*
Chief Creative Officer: *Joani Schultz*
Assistant Editor: *Janis Sampson*

Book Designer/Illustrator: *Jean Bruns*
Print Production Artist: *Tracy K. Hindman*
Cover Art Director/Designer: *Jeff A. Storm*
Production Manager: *Dodie Tipton*

Unless otherwise noted, Scripture taken from the HOLY BIBLE, NEW INTERNATIONAL VERSION®. Copyright © 1973, 1978, 1984 by International Bible Society. Used by permission of Zondervan Publishing House. All rights reserved.

LIBRARY OF CONGRESS CATALOGING-IN-PUBLICATION DATA
Belknap, Bryan.
Group's blockbuster movie illustrations : the sequel.
     p. cm.
   Includes indexes.
   ISBN 0-7644-2454-8 (pbk. : alk. paper)
   1. Motion pictures in Christian education. 2. Christian education of teenagers.
   I. Group Publishing. II. Title.
BV1535.4.B45 2003
268'.67--dc21

                                                              2002156649

10 9 8 7 6 5 4 3 2 1   12 11 10 09 08 07 06 05 04 03
Printed in the United States of America.

CONTENTS

DEDICATION

Thank you to my precious bride, Jill, for putting up with
all the movies,

to Rick and Kathy for always encouraging me,

to Kelli for helping me sound cogent,

and to Thom and Joani Schultz for believing in me.

INTRODUCTION

Jesus practiced the art of grabbing and holding listener attention. He used stories wrapped in everyday life that revealed deep spiritual truth. You want to do the same, right? So you dazzle your youth with tales of farms, seeds, and swine.

I think not.

You've all heard the urban legend about the eager young youth pastor, exuberant about getting jiggy and offering a fresh perspective to his students on eternal truth. He decided to ditch the trite anecdotes and cheesy allegories. He was determined to speak in the language of the school halls and the streets by jumping into the trenches and connecting with the audience. He turned his baseball hat sideways, rolled up one pant leg, and turned Psalms...into a rap.

I heard the funeral was lovely.

I know it's only legend. But every pastor knows how hard it can be sometimes to come up with an innovative tool to spark discussion and capture attention. Unfortunately, the impromptu dog and pony show typically lands behind Popsicle-stick crafts on the cutting-edge scale. Save some time (and your pride) with video clips! *Group's Blockbuster Movie Illustrations: The Sequel* offers over 170 priceless teachable moments from more than one hundred of Hollywood's greatest hits, from classics like *Dead Poets Society* and *Home Alone* to more recent flicks such as *The Lord of the Rings: The Fellowship of the Ring* and *A Walk to Remember*.

Jesus used parables, a popular form of entertainment in his day, to impart spiritual truth to the masses. Modern audiences now turn to movies for their mass entertainment. *Group's Blockbuster Movie Illustrations: The Sequel* points out film clips (modern society's "parables") that powerfully portray biblical truth. Relate everyday life to God's eternal Word by using these scenes in youth talks, devotions, small-group meetings, retreats, lessons, and even Sunday morning sermons! This easy-to-use collection of illustrations covers 290 crucial youth ministry topics, such as body image, materialism, and self-control. Using film as a spiritual reference point not only connects with seasoned Christians but also speaks to unchurched seekers in a language they understand.

How to Use *Group's Blockbuster Movie Illustrations: The Sequel*

Do you have a key point or a specific Scripture passage that you'd like to illustrate? Since the clips are organized by topic, simply flip to the themes that tie in with your main point, or select a clip using the Scripture Index. Once you've picked a clip, you'll find that the illustration is divided into several parts. Each movie illustration begins by introducing the theme, title, and rating information of the movie, and includes a Scripture passage that relates to the theme. You'll also discover...

Funny/Dramatic Icons—An icon is shown at the beginning of each clip to let you know if the tone of the movie clip is humorous or dramatic.

Alternate Takes—Though the discussion questions focus on a specific theme, each of the clips in this book could be used to spark discussions on a variety of topics. Alternate Takes provide additional themes and Scriptures that you could use to start discussions.

Start Time/End Time—These times tell you when to start and stop the tape. Clip locations are determined by setting the tape counter on your VCR or DVD player to 00:00:00 when the studio logo for the film appears (immediately before the opening credits). All Start/End Times are approximated to the closest 15-second interval.

Start Cue/End Cue—If you have an unreliable timer on your VCR, these visual cues specify the action or dialogue that takes place at the beginning and end of each clip.

Duration—Here you'll get an estimate of the elapsed time of each clip. To keep the focus on the point you want to illustrate and not turn the clip into a full-blown screening, every movie clip is three minutes or less.

Overview—Here you'll get the scoop on the action of the clip and the names of the main characters. To find out more about the plot of the entire movie, check out the details included in the Movie Background Index (pp. 141-151).

Illustration—What's the point? This is the place to look for a brief explanation of the spiritual significance of the clip and how it relates to teenagers' lives. Feel free to use it as a guide, and then explain the main point in your own words.

Questions—Need some discussion starters? Here you'll find questions that break the ice, dig into the truth of Scripture, and help kids apply that truth to their lives. Remember, if you're using an Alternate Take, you'll need to come up with your own discussion questions that apply to the theme you've chosen.

After you've previewed the clip and cued the tape to the Start Time, you're ready to dive in! Just make sure you pay attention to a few important details.

Copyright Laws—Believe it or not, the FBI warning at the beginning of most videos is for real! In general, federal copyright laws do not allow you to use videos (even ones you own) for any purpose other than home viewing. Though narrow exceptions exist for using short segments of copyrighted material in church, it's best to be completely legal. Your church can obtain a license from the Motion Picture Licensing Corporation for a small fee. Just visit www.mplc.com or call 1-800-462-8855 for more information. When using a movie that is not covered by the license, you should directly contact the movie studio to seek permission for use of the clip.

Content—Go ahead and sigh with relief…*Group's Blockbuster Movie Illustrations: The Sequel* contains absolutely no clips from R-rated movies! As you know, even many PG and PG-13 movies contain inappropriate or offensive content. Be sensitive to the fact that some students may view your use of a clip as an endorsement of the entire movie. Do some research! Read the Movie Background Index to find a summary of the plot, and use resources such as the Internet to get a better idea of questionable themes or content. Sometimes it may be necessary to voice a disclaimer, letting students know that, although you value the scene you're showing, you do not approve of the rest of the movie. (For information on illustrations from R-rated films, such as *Black Hawk Down, The Green Mile,* and *The Matrix,* visit Group's movie clip database at www.ministryandmedia.com.)

I've been very careful (and my editor has checked twice) to recommend clips free of questionable content, though the same guarantee can't be made for the scenes before or after the suggested clip. The most important principle to remember is this: **Preview the clips!** Be careful with VCRs that roll back several seconds when stopped! Make sure you've got the timing just right so that you don't have to spend the next year apologizing for an unfortunate mistake.

Parents—Of course, you can't even think about exposing your youth to something without considering their parents first. Pre-empt the closed-door, full-of-shouting meeting with "Mr. Smith" by sending students home with a permission slip before you start showing movie clips. You don't need anything fancy or written in blood, but a simple "here's what's up" should suffice, so they know you haven't joined the cult of cinema. Try something like...

> *Jesus taught deep spiritual truth with examples from everyday life. The modern parallel to Jesus' parables is film. In an effort to connect teenagers' everyday life with their faith while illustrating spiritual matters in a concrete way they will grasp, I would like to use movie clips as illustrations during our youth events.*
>
> *Every clip is carefully screened and contains no objectionable content. The clips will be three minutes or less so the focus always remains on God's Word and never the movie itself. My prayer is to bring Scripture alive and get your young people thinking about their faith outside the church walls by using these clips.*
>
> *Please contact me with any questions or concerns about showing movie clips in the youth ministry. Please sign below if you have no objections. Thank you for your time and your trust with your child's spiritual growth!*

Now you're ready to go! Dim the lights, pass around the ultra-fattening popcorn, press "play" on the VCR, and dive deep with your kids into the issues hidden below the surface of the screen. You'll be amazed at the life-changing discussions that will result from even the cheesiest movies, and you'll be thankful that watching movie clips can actually spur your teenagers on to pursue Jesus!

The
MOVIE ILLUSTRATION
Themes

Abandonment | DON'T LEAVE!

Title: A.I.: ARTIFICIAL INTELLIGENCE (PG-13)
Warner Bros., 2001

Scripture: Genesis 16:3-13

Alternate Take: Teaching Children (Deuteronomy 11:18)

START TIME:	49 minutes, 30 seconds
START CUE:	David spreads out a blanket.
END TIME:	52 minutes, 15 seconds
END CUE:	Mom speeds away in the car.
DURATION:	2 minutes, 45 seconds

Overview: Mom leaves David in the forest. David pleads and cries for her not to leave him. Mom warns David about where not to go, apologizes for not teaching him more, and abandons him.

Illustration: Unfortunately, this scene will probably hit too close to home for many people who have felt abandoned by their loved ones. Use this discussion to help your young people recover from scars of abandonment, leading them to the healing love of their heavenly Father who will never leave or forsake them.

Questions
- **Have you ever felt abandoned? What happened?**
- **How did being abandoned affect you?**
  Read aloud Genesis 16:3-13.
- **Why does God care about abandoned people?**
- **How can you find comfort in God when you feel abandoned?**

Acceptance | WILL YOU BE MY FRIEND?

Title: FINDING FORRESTER (PG-13)
Columbia Pictures, 2000

Scripture: Matthew 5:14-16

Alternate Take: Talents (Matthew 25:14-29)

START TIME:	9 minutes, 15 seconds
START CUE:	Mrs. Wallace sits with Jamal's teacher.
END TIME:	10 minutes, 30 seconds
END CUE:	Their meeting ends.
DURATION:	1 minute, 15 seconds

Overview: Jamal's teacher explains that his standardized test scores are phenomenal, but he only turns in average schoolwork. Unfortunately, Jamal won't do anything to stand out in the classroom, only on the basketball court because that's where he gains acceptance.

Illustration: Everyone wants acceptance. (Even antisocial people find others to be antisocial with!) Problems arise when people hide or repress their faith in God in an effort to gain approval. Use this clip to encourage teenagers to place their relationship with God above the temporal acceptance of their peers.

Questions
- **What are some common things people do to gain acceptance?**
- **Have you ever hidden something about yourself so people would accept you? What happened?**

Read aloud Matthew 5:14-16.

- **What reasons do people have for hiding their faith?**
- **How can you display your faith in the future and still find acceptance from your peers?**

Addiction | I CAN QUIT ANYTIME

Title: THE LORD OF THE RINGS:
THE FELLOWSHIP OF THE RING (PG-13)
New Line Cinema, 2001

Scripture: Philippians 3:17-19

Alternate Take: Rebuke (Matthew 18:15-17)

START TIME:	20 minutes, 45 seconds
START CUE:	Bilbo crosses to the fireplace.
END TIME:	23 minutes, 45 seconds
END CUE:	Bilbo walks outside.
DURATION:	3 minutes

Overview: Bilbo grapples with leaving his magic ring to Frodo, unable to tear himself away from it. Gandalf shocks Bilbo into relinquishing the ring, breaking the spell it holds over his little friend.

Illustration: Bilbo exhibits all the classic signs of an addict—the knowledge that his "habit" destroys him and a complete inability to give it up. Discuss addiction, its genesis, symptoms, and consequences as well as how the redemptive power of Jesus Christ can break addiction's crushing grip.

Questions

- **How is Bilbo's need for the ring an addiction?**
- **What are some common addictions, and what makes them difficult to break?**

Read aloud Philippians 3:17-19.

- **How can someone's appetite be their "god"? How does this passage relate to addictions?**
- **How can you protect yourself from addictions? How can you minister to someone who is addicted?**

Alcohol | IT EASES THE PAIN

Title: THE MAJESTIC (PG)
Warner Bros., 2001

Scripture: Proverbs 20:1

Alternate Takes: Depression (2 Corinthians 1:8-9),
Trials (2 Thessalonians 1:3-5)

START TIME:	11 minutes, 00 seconds
START CUE:	Pete pours a drink.
END TIME:	13 minutes, 30 seconds
END CUE:	Pete exits with the monkey.
DURATION:	2 minutes, 30 seconds

Overview: Pete moans to the bartender about his woes with the government, his derailed screenwriting career, and his ex-girlfriend. He leaves the bar to drive home, obviously drunk.

Illustration: Far too many people seek to change their personalities or run from their problems through alcohol. Use this scene to jump beyond the petty moral and social issues straight to the heart of alcohol abuse.

Questions

- **What reasons do people have for drinking alcohol?**
- **Does alcohol ever help people with their problems and fears? Why or why not?**

Read aloud Proverbs 20:1.

- **What are the ways alcohol leads people astray?**
- **How can God help a person with the problems they try to escape through alcohol?**

Anger | SLAP YOU SILLY

Title: MY DOG SKIP (PG)
Warner Bros., 2000

Scripture: Psalm 37:7-9

Alternate Takes: Violence (Genesis 4:1-8), Animals (Psalm 8)

START TIME:	1 hour, 6 minutes, 45 seconds
START CUE:	Willie blows the play.
END TIME:	1 hour, 9 minutes, 15 seconds
END CUE:	Rivers gets up to leave.
DURATION:	2 minutes, 30 seconds

Overview: Willie blows a play in his baseball game and everyone in the stands starts laughing at him. His dog Skip runs out on the field, trying to cheer him up. Willie gets so angry that he slaps Skip violently.

Illustration: Anger must be dealt with and controlled before it not only turns into sin but also spills onto innocent bystanders. Discuss this clip to help your youth deal with anger constructively.

Questions

- **Why do people take their anger out on others who don't deserve it?**
- **How do you usually deal with your anger?**
  Read aloud Psalm 37:7-9.
- **How can you "be still before the Lord" when you're angry?**
- **What are some constructive ways to deal with feelings of anger?**

Annoying People | WHAT WOULD JESUS DO?

Title: SHREK (PG)
DreamWorks SKG, 2001

Scripture: Proverbs 27:14

Alternate Takes: Friends (Ecclesiastes 4:9-12), Prejudice (Exodus 23:9)

START TIME:	7 minutes, 30 seconds
START CUE:	Donkey asks, "Can I say something?"
END TIME:	10 minutes, 00 seconds
END CUE:	Donkey says, "You all right."
DURATION:	2 minutes, 30 seconds

Overview: Shrek tells Donkey to go with his friends. Donkey doesn't have any friends, so he decides to hang out with Shrek. Shrek tells Donkey to stop following him because he's an ogre. When Shrek asks, "Doesn't that bother you?" Donkey shrugs and says, "Nope."

Illustration: There's one in every person's life—that annoying guy or gal who drives you crazy. Believe it or not, these loud, obnoxious, and grating people are loved by the One who created them in his image. We should love them, too. Use this scene to start a discussion about ways to not just tolerate the difficult people God places in one's life, but to appreciate them as God's children.

Questions

- **What traits make a person annoying to you?**
  Read aloud Proverbs 27:14.
- **How would you normally react to a person like this?**
- **Why are we supposed to love annoying people?**
- **How can you show love and kindness to a person without being their best friend?**

Appearances | LOOKS CAN DECEIVE

Title: MEN IN BLACK (PG-13)
Columbia Pictures, 1997

Scripture: John 7:21-24
Alternate Take: Animals (Hebrews 2:6-8)

START TIME:	1 hour, 6 minutes, 15 seconds
START CUE:	A dog and freak man stand at a shop.
END TIME:	1 hour, 7 minutes, 45 seconds
END CUE:	J releases the dog.
DURATION:	1 minute, 30 seconds

Overview: K comments on the alien's terrible disguise until Frank the dog speaks up. J interrogates the dog, who confesses that the universe they are looking for is on Earth. They can't believe billions of stars could be on their planet, but Frank insists that looks can be deceiving.

Illustration: It's easy to make assumptions based on appearances. Use this discussion to challenge your young people to stop making decisions based solely on a person's or situation's appearance.

Questions

- **Have you ever misjudged someone based on his or her appearance? What happened?**

- **Why do we naturally categorize people by outward appearances?**
  Read aloud John 7:21-24.
- **How does looking at appearances cause a person to miss "God-opportunities"?**
- **What do you need to change in order to start looking beyond appearances?**

Atonement | TAKE ME

Title: BROKEDOWN PALACE (PG-13)
20th Century Fox, 1999

Scripture: Romans 5:6-11

Alternate Takes: Confession (Psalm 51:1-7),
Friendship (John 15:12-13)

START TIME:	1 hour, 28 minutes, 00 seconds
START CUE:	The cops grab Darlene.
END TIME:	1 hour, 31 minutes, 00 seconds
END CUE:	Alice leaves the court.
DURATION:	3 minutes

Overview: Alice runs to the judge and claims Darlene is innocent. Alice claims that she hasn't been a good friend and says *she* was the one who smuggled the drugs. Alice says it is all her mistake and offers to take Darlene's punishment on top of her own. The judge doesn't know whether to believe her, but accepts her bargain.

Illustration: What a gripping picture of how Jesus substituted himself on our behalf! He took our punishment on himself through his death on the cross so that we could be set free from the punishment we deserve. Use this scene to start a discussion about how Jesus is our atoning sacrifice.

Questions
- **What would motivate someone to take another person's punishment?**
  Read aloud Romans 5:6-11.
- **Why did Jesus take our punishment for sin upon himself?**
- **Why did Jesus become a substitute for people he knew would never love or follow him?**
- **How can we show Jesus gratitude for his act of atonement?**

Attitude | YOU CAN'T HIDE IT

Title: REMEMBER THE TITANS (PG)
Walt Disney Productions, 2000

Scripture: 1 Chronicles 28:9

Alternate Takes: Leadership (1 Peter 5:1-4),
Teamwork (Ecclesiastes 4:9-12)

START TIME:	29 minutes, 15 seconds
START CUE:	Gerry and Julius bump into each other.
END TIME:	30 minutes, 45 seconds
END CUE:	Julius says, "Attitude reflect leadership, captain."
DURATION:	1 minute, 30 seconds

Overview: Gerry berates Julius for not listening and not sacrificing for the team. Julius responds, saying that leaders must lead, and he accuses Gerry of not guiding the white players to sacrifice for their black teammates. Gerry shakes his head at Julius' poor attitude.

Illustration: We can go through the motions in life, but we can't hide the attitude behind our actions. God cares about the hearts and attitudes of his children. Use this scene to run an attitude check with your students.

Questions

- **What usually happens when you do something with a bad attitude?**
- **Where does a person's attitude come from, and how can it be changed?** Read aloud 1 Chronicles 28:9.
- **Do obedient actions done with a bad attitude please God? Why or why not?**
- **What attitude adjustments do you need to make in your life, and how can you do that?**

Authority | I'M UNDER WHOSE?

Title: THE FIFTH ELEMENT (PG-13)
Columbia Pictures, 1997

Scripture: Romans 13:1-5

Alternate Take: Helping Others (Proverbs 14:31)

START TIME:	34 minutes, 00 seconds
START CUE:	The police address Korben.
END TIME:	36 minutes, 15 seconds
END CUE:	Korben says, "This is so stupid."
DURATION:	2 minutes, 15 seconds

Overview: Korben explains all the reasons he can't help Leeloo escape the police. She begs him one last time, and Korben gives in, ignoring the orders of the police as he speeds away.

Illustration: Many people have authority over us: familial authorities, governmental authorities, and spiritual authorities, for example. Use this discussion to help your young people understand why God places authority figures in our lives, why we should submit to them, and when it's OK to disobey them.

Questions

- **Who are some authority figures in your life?**
  Read aloud Romans 13:1-5.
- **What makes it difficult to submit to an authority?**
- **How does submitting to others teach us to be more like Christ?**
- **How should a person respond to authorities he or she doesn't agree with?**
- **Can you ever disobey an authority in your life? If so, when?**

Belief | I'M ABSOLUTELY SURE...I THINK

Title: MISSION: IMPOSSIBLE (PG-13)
Paramount Pictures, 1996

Scripture: Mark 9:17-24

Alternate Takes: Faith (2 Corinthians 5:7), Doubts (James 1:5-8)

START TIME:	1 hour, 13 minutes, 15 seconds
START CUE:	Krieger enters the room.
END TIME:	1 hour, 15 minutes, 30 seconds
END CUE:	Krieger exits the room.
DURATION:	2 minutes, 15 seconds

Overview: Krieger blackmails Ethan with the computer disk. Ethan produces the real computer disk, playing sleight of hand by making it appear and disappear. Krieger storms out, convinced he has the wrong disk.

Illustration: One's beliefs can often shift when confronted with new information or persuasion. God doesn't want his kids blowin' in the wind, so use this discussion to offer some rock-solid anchor points on which teenagers can fasten their beliefs.

Questions

- **How did Ethan sway Krieger's beliefs about the disk?**
- **What do you consider to be your core beliefs, and how have people tried to sway you?**
  Read aloud Mark 9:17-24.

- **What are some faith issues you find hard to believe?**
- **How will knowing what you believe help you in everyday life?**

Bible Study | YOU WANT ME TO READ?

Title: LEGALLY BLONDE (PG-13)
MGM, 2001

Scripture: Psalm 1

Alternate Takes: Readiness (Luke 12:43-48),
Mercy (Matthew 23:23)

START TIME:	27 minutes, 00 seconds
START CUE:	Professor Stromwell says, "I assume all of you have read..."
END TIME:	28 minutes, 45 seconds
END CUE:	Elle leaves class.
DURATION:	1 minute, 45 seconds

Overview: Professor Stromwell asks Elle a question, and she responds by saying she didn't know she was supposed to read anything. Professor Stromwell asks a class member if it's acceptable for Miss Woods to be unprepared. Miss Kensington responds "no," and says that Elle should leave class.

Illustration: Though God doesn't kick us out of class for not reading his Word, this clip can start a valuable discussion on the importance of studying the Bible. So many Christians respond like deer in the headlights when they're questioned about the Bible, the very book they claim to place complete faith in as the divinely inspired Word of God. Challenge teenagers in your ministry to start cramming for "class" and learning the Word.

Questions
- **If we had a pop quiz on the Bible right now, how would you do?**
- **What things keep you from reading the Bible more often?**
  Read aloud Psalm 1.
- **How can knowing God's Word help in difficult or surprising situations?**
- **Does a person have to read the Bible to be a follower of Christ? Explain.**
- **How can you make reading the Bible a part of your daily routine?**

Body Image | I HATE MY MIRROR

Title: ZOOLANDER (PG-13)
Paramount Pictures, 2001

Scripture: 1 Peter 3:3-4

Alternate Takes: Eating Disorders (1 Corinthians 6:19-20), Media Messages (Proverbs 2:6-12)

START TIME:	58 minutes, 30 seconds
START CUE:	Zoolander asks, "Why do you hate models, Matilda?"
END TIME:	1 hour, 00 minutes, 30 seconds
END CUE:	Zoolander asks, "You can read minds?"
DURATION:	2 minutes

Overview: Matilda reveals that her deep hatred for models stems from her obesity in seventh grade and how inadequate she felt when looking at women in magazines. The only way she could try to be thin and beautiful like them was to become bulimic.

Illustration: I'll let you in on a dirty Hollywood secret: The beautiful people you see on TV and in magazines *don't exist*! They're all products of airbrushing and Photoshop. Use this scene to encourage teenagers to use God's standards for beauty and not the world's self-esteem-damaging pipe dreams.

Questions
- **How does the media affect our standards for beauty?**
- **How do you measure your appearance compared to what is presented in the media? compared to your peers?**
  Read aloud 1 Peter 3:3-4.
- **What is God's standard for beauty?**
- **What changes could you make so you derive your self-image from God's standards, not the media?**

The Bride of Christ | I DO

Title: A WALK TO REMEMBER (PG)
Warner Bros., 2002

Scripture: Ephesians 5:25-27

Alternate Takes: Love (1 Corinthians 13),
Marriage (Genesis 2:20-24)

START TIME:	1 hour, 32 minutes, 30 seconds
START CUE:	The exterior of the church is shown.
END TIME:	1 hour, 34 minutes, 45 seconds
END CUE:	Jamie and Landon exchange rings.
DURATION:	2 minutes, 15 seconds

Overview: Jamie and Landon get married, taking their " 'til death do us part" vows after Jamie's dad reads 1 Corinthians 13.

Illustration: The Bible often describes the church as the "bride of Christ." This clip provides a visual context for this highly intimate spiritual truth. Use it to challenge students to consider what their relationship with God is meant to be like.

Questions

- **How does this scene make you feel?**
  Read aloud Ephesians 5:25-27.
- **Why does Paul refer to the church as Jesus' "bride"?**
- **What responsibilities come with being the bride of Christ?**
- **What can you do to move closer to becoming a spotless bride?**

Change | I DON'T WANT TO LEAVE

Title: SUPERMAN (PG)
Warner Bros., 1978

Scripture: Hebrews 5:11-14

Alternate Take: Abraham (Genesis 12:1-4)

START TIME:	39 minutes, 00 seconds
START CUE:	Ma approaches Clark in the field.
END TIME:	40 minutes, 45 seconds
END CUE:	Clark and Ma hug.
DURATION:	1 minute, 45 seconds

Overview: Clark tells Ma he has to leave. He doesn't know exactly where he's headed, but he feels he must leave (even though he *wants* to stay).

Illustration: Change can be a scary prospect. Everyone has to change—whether it means changing from a teenager to an adult, a sinner into a child of God, or going from life to death. Challenge your young people to make the changes necessary to mature in their faith, no matter how frightened they may be of the growth process.

Questions

- What is the most difficult change you've ever had to make?
- Why is change so difficult?

Read aloud Hebrews 5:11-14.

- Why is change a necessary component of maturity?
- What changes do you need to make in order to move closer to spiritual maturity?

Chaos | ORDER IN THE COURT

Title: JURASSIC PARK (PG-13)
Universal Pictures, 1993

Scripture: Colossians 1:16-17

Alternate Takes: Order (Isaiah 48:12-13), God's Control (Daniel 4:35)

START TIME:	46 minutes, 45 seconds
START CUE:	Dr. Grant puts on his hat.
END TIME:	48 minutes, 45 seconds
END CUE:	Malcolm says, "That's chaos theory."
DURATION:	2 minutes

Overview: Malcolm explains chaos theory to Dr. Sattler by dripping water on her hand. He notes how the water rolls in different directions when it's placed in the same spot in an effort to prove that one can't predict everything. Dr. Grant unexpectedly jumps out of the car, and Malcolm claims that's proof of chaos theory.

Illustration: Life can sometimes feel completely random, as Malcolm suggests in this clip. Help students see that God, however, is the true source of order in the apparent social and environmental chaos of the world.

Questions

- Where do you see evidence of chaos around you?
- Why does the universe naturally move toward chaos instead of order?

Read aloud Colossians 1:16-17.

- Do you see evidence of God holding everything together? If so, where?
- How has God calmed the chaos in your own life?

Title: THE CIDER HOUSE RULES (PG-13)
Miramax Films, 1999

Scripture: Ephesians 1:3-6

Alternate Takes: Orphans (Deuteronomy 24:19-21),
God's Love (Psalm 36:5-9)

START TIME:	13 minutes, 45 seconds
START CUE:	The couple arrives at the orphanage.
END TIME:	15 minutes, 45 seconds
END CUE:	Curly takes comfort that someone asked about him.
DURATION:	2 minutes

Overview: A couple arrives at the orphanage to choose a child, and they pick a little girl. Curly gets upset because he feels as if no one wants him. Homer comforts him, saying that Dr. Larch won't let just *anyone* take him because he is so special.

Illustration: It's amazing that the perfect Creator of the universe adopts broken and sinful children into his heavenly family—but it's true. While we may hear the words "children of God" a lot, use this clip to bring home the emotion involved in being chosen and adopted by our spiritual Father.

Questions
• **What makes a person a "child of God"?**
  Read aloud Ephesians 1:3-6.
• **What makes adoption by God so special?**
• **What rights do God's children receive?**
• **How should a child of God live?**

Christmas | WHATZIT ALL MEAN?

Title: DR. SUESS' HOW THE GRINCH
STOLE CHRISTMAS (PG)
Universal Pictures, 2000

Scripture: Luke 2:1-20

Alternate Take: Trials (James 1:2-4)

START TIME:	1 hour, 19 minutes, 30 seconds
START CUE:	The mayor says, "Well, I wonder who could've done this."
END TIME:	1 hour, 21 minutes, 45 seconds
END CUE:	The mayor says, "Awww, give me a break."
DURATION:	2 minutes, 15 seconds

Overview: The mayor blames the Grinch for destroying Christmas. Mr. Lou Who steps forward and claims that he's glad the Grinch stole their presents. It reminded him that Christmas isn't about the gifts and contests but about family.

Illustration: It sure is easy to lose sight of the real reason for the season. Use this clip to take the focus one step further, helping teenagers see that Christmas isn't just about family, it's about the Son of God lying in a manger.

Questions

- **What do you think of when you hear the word** *Christmas?* Read aloud Luke 2:1-20.
- **What's the true meaning of Christmas?**
- **What are some things that distract people from the true meaning of Christmas?**
- **How can you keep Jesus at the center of your Christmas experience this year?**

The Church | GOD LIVES IN HERE

Title: A KNIGHT'S TALE (PG-13)
Columbia Pictures, 2001

Scripture: Ephesians 5:25-32
Alternate Takes: Beauty (Proverbs 6:25-26),
Serving God (Matthew 6:22-24)

START TIME:	22 minutes, 00 seconds
START CUE:	William asks, "Would you speak to me?"
END TIME:	24 minutes, 00 seconds
END CUE:	The bishop leaves, singing.
DURATION:	2 minutes

Overview: William accidentally rides his horse into church while flirting with Jocelyn. Naturally, the bishop flips when he discovers a horse desecrating the church! The bishop sputters, "Does this not shock you?!" Jocelyn apologizes, claiming she could better serve God without the curse of beauty.

23

Illustration: Churches struggle with what constitutes "acceptable behavior" within their walls. Use this scene to examine church tradition and to explore what are some good criteria for discerning between the sacred and sacrilege.

Questions
- **Why do many people view a church building as sacred?**
  Read aloud Ephesians 5:25-32.
- **What is our personal responsibility as the "church"?**
- **How does God determine what is acceptable behavior inside a church building?**
- **Is there anything you think we should add or subtract from our church service? Explain.**

Cliques | DON'T CROSS THAT LINE

Title: CAN'T BUY ME LOVE (PG-13)
Touchstone Pictures, 1987

Scripture: Psalm 133

Alternate Take: Popularity (2 Samuel 15:1-6)

START TIME:	7 minutes, 00 seconds
START CUE:	Ronald and Kenneth carry their books.
END TIME:	8 minutes, 00 seconds
END CUE:	Ronald says, "At our own school."
DURATION:	1 minute

Overview: Ronald and Kenneth talk about popularity and cliques. Ronald wants to hang out with the popular kids, but Kenneth says it will never happen.

Illustration: Christians can't opt for cliques. God desires unity among his people, which leaves cliques out of the question. Use this scene to challenge teenagers in your group to tear down the walls of cliques and open up their lives to all types of people.

Questions
- **What are the cliques in your school? in our group?**
- **What are the benefits of cliques? the dangers?**
  Read aloud Psalm 133.
- **What makes "living together in unity" so "pleasant"?**
- **How can cliques destroy unity?**
- **What are some ways we can break down the walls of cliques and create unity?**

Comfort Zone | WHERE'S MY SUITCASE?

Title: CHICKEN RUN (G)
DreamWorks SKG, 2000

Scripture: Genesis 12:1-5
Alternate Takes: Freedom (John 8:31-36),
Israel in Egypt (Exodus 5:1-21)

START TIME:	16 minutes, 30 seconds
START CUE:	Ginger says, "Think, everyone, think."
END TIME:	18 minutes, 00 seconds
END CUE:	The door closes behind Ginger.
DURATION:	1 minute, 30 seconds

Overview: Ginger longs for freedom while her friends are content laying eggs and getting fed. She paints a verbal picture of trees, grass, and freedom, but her friends would rather remain in captivity.

Illustration: God calls us to leave our comfort zones and step out in faith. Many people refuse to move because they've erected barriers in their minds, believing that "blessed" people live in comfort and security. (Where does that leave Mother Teresa?) Use this discussion to challenge teenagers' safe lifestyles and encourage the dramatic spiritual growth that leads others to the freedom that Christ offers.

Questions

- **What things in your life make up your "comfort zone"?**
  Read aloud Genesis 12:1-5.
- **Why didn't God give Abram more details?**
- **Why might God want a person to leave a safe, comfortable place or position in life?**
- **How can a person gain the courage to obey God, even if it means leaving his or her comfort zone?**

Community | GATHER 'ROUND

Title: MEN IN BLACK (PG-13)
Columbia Pictures, 1997

Scripture: Luke 14:16-23
Alternate Take: Tests (Psalm 94:19)

START TIME:	25 minutes, 30 seconds
START CUE:	The recruits tear open their tests.
END TIME:	27 minutes, 00 seconds
END CUE:	The recruits stare at Edwards.
DURATION:	1 minute, 30 seconds

Overview: Everyone takes a test while sitting inside incredibly uncomfortable chairs. Finally, Edwards drags a coffee table over to write on and invites everyone to join him around it.

Illustration: Too often we're running around in our own little world doing our own little thing instead of seeking ways to build community with the people beside us. This clip can help students brainstorm ways to create a greater sense of community in your ministry.

Questions

- **What are some ways that people create a sense of community?**
- **Do we do a good job of inviting people to "gather 'round" the table with us? Why or why not?**
Read aloud Luke 14:16-23.
- **What are some ways to actually create community between different types of people?**
- **How can we make this group more welcoming for new people?**

Compassion | GET OFF MY PORCH!

Title: SHREK (PG)
DreamWorks SKG, 2001

Scripture: 1 John 3:14-17

Alternate Takes: Community (Joshua 7:1-13), Hospitality (Luke 11:5-10)

START TIME:	12 minutes, 45 seconds
START CUE:	Shrek says, "I thought I told you to stay outside."
END TIME:	15 minutes, 30 seconds
END CUE:	Shrek says, "You're coming with me."
DURATION:	2 minutes, 45 seconds

Overview: Shrek enters his house and finds three blind mice, seven dwarves, one comatose Snow White, and a wolf dressed as Grandma. He kicks everyone out and discovers that his swamp is infested with fairy tale creatures who've been displaced by Lord Farquaad.

Illustration: Helping others who are in need doesn't usually fit neatly into our plans. Yet Christians shouldn't turn a blind eye to those who need help. Use this scene to help your young people figure out ways to show compassion toward those who unexpectedly invade their "swamp," seeking help.

Questions

- **What factors can make showing compassion difficult?**
  Read aloud 1 John 3:14-17.
- **Why is it our Christian duty to have compassion on people in need?**
- **What are the spiritual consequences of not helping others?**
- **Are we required to say yes to every request for help? If not, how do you decide?**
- **Who needs your compassion this week, and how can you show it?**

Competition | ALL ABOUT ME

Title: RAT RACE (PG-13)
Paramount Pictures, 2001

Scripture: Philippians 2:3-8

Alternate Take: Gambling (1 Timothy 6:17-19)

START TIME:	22 minutes, 30 seconds
START CUE:	The racers run down the stairs.
END TIME:	24 minutes, 00 seconds
END CUE:	Sinclair says, "My casino is where…"
DURATION:	1 minute, 30 seconds

Overview: The racers run down the stairs and collapse in a heap. Owen suggests that they work together and split the money. They agree until Enrico runs by them, working on his own. Donald Sinclair and the gamblers watch the competitors on television monitors.

Illustration: Too many people buy into the dog-eat-dog, survival of the fittest mentality depicted in this clip. This attitude contradicts Jesus' teachings of caring for the weak and helping others get ahead before seeking your own self-interests. Use this clip to challenge the prevalent self-centered worldview, and present God's plan that the fittest should help others survive.

Questions

- **What factors make our society so competitive?**
  Read aloud Philippians 2:3-8.
- **Does this Scripture passage mean Christians can't compete?**
  Why or why not?

- How can a person look out for others and still care for himself or herself?
- How do you need to become more aware of others' needs in your own everyday life?

Compliments | YOUR DRESS ISN'T *THAT* UGLY...

Title: AS GOOD AS IT GETS (PG-13)
TriStar Pictures, 1997

Scripture: Ephesians 4:29
Alternate Take: Taming the Tongue (Proverbs 10:21)

START TIME:	1 hour, 37 minutes, 30 seconds
START CUE:	Melvin sits.
END TIME:	1 hour, 40 minutes, 30 seconds
END CUE:	Melvin says, "You make me want to be a better man."
DURATION:	3 minutes

Overview: Melvin insults Carol's dress. She threatens to leave unless he gives her a compliment. He struggles to come up with something, and finally lands a doozy.

Illustration: Compliments are a lost art in a society that lauds quick-cutting tongues. God obviously isn't with the times since he commands his children to always build others up. Use this clip to help teenagers make the seismic shift from cut-downs to compliments.

Questions
- What was the last compliment you received, and how did it make you feel?
- Do you find it difficult to compliment someone? Why or why not?
  Read aloud Ephesians 4:29.
- Why do people generally tear others down instead of build them up?
- How would giving people only compliments change your life and the lives of others?

Confession | NO REALLY, I LIKE THE RAIN.

Title: THE WINSLOW BOY (G)
Sony Pictures Classics, 1999

Scripture: 1 John 1:8-10

Alternate Takes: God's Compassion (Nehemiah 9:17-20),
Truth (Proverbs 12:22)

START TIME:	22 minutes, 15 seconds
START CUE:	Ronnie enters his father's office.
END TIME:	24 minutes, 00 seconds
END CUE:	Mr. Winslow stares at his son.
DURATION:	1 minute, 45 seconds

Overview: Ronnie Winslow approaches his father, soaked to the bone from standing in the rain. Ronnie fears his father's rejection when he learns about his
expulsion. Mr. Winslow guarantees he won't be angry as long as Ronnie tells
the truth, warning that he'll see through any lies.

Illustration: This clip is a stirring portrait of what it can be like to stand before
our heavenly Father. Sometimes we fear confessing our failures, but our Father
beckons us inside with open arms. Encourage your young people to receive
God's forgiveness and peace by coming out of the rain and confessing their sins
to their loving Father.

Questions

• **Did you ever try to hide something from your parents as a child? What
happened?**
Read aloud 1 John 1:8-10.

• **What can make confessing a sin to God seem frightening?**

• **What are the benefits of confessing sin?**

• **Is there anything you need to confess to God today? If so, what's holding
you back?**

Confrontation | PLEASE LISTEN TO ME!

Title: TWISTER (PG-13)
Warner Bros., 1996

Scripture: Leviticus 19:17

Alternate Takes: Friends (Proverbs 27:9-10),
Consequences (Proverbs 21:16), Rebuke (Matthew 18:15-17)

START TIME:	1 hour, 31 minutes, 45 seconds
START CUE:	Jonas says, "We're right along side her."
END TIME:	1 hour, 34 minutes, 15 seconds
END CUE:	Jo says, "We tried."
DURATION:	2 minutes, 30 seconds

Overview: Jo warns Jonas about the danger of his proximity to the twister. Jonas disregards her advice and suffers fatal consequences for ignoring wise counsel.

Illustration: Many people will stand by and watch their friends crash and burn because of foolish choices. They won't say anything because they feel it's "none of their business." We must learn to lovingly confront others with their sin, helping them see the truth of a situation before they suffer the harmful consequences.

Questions

- **Is it hard for you to confront others? Why or why not?**
Read aloud Leviticus 19:17.
- **Why are we responsible for confronting our Christian brothers and sisters?**
- **What are some tactful ways to confront a person?**
- **What should you do if the person you confront doesn't listen to you?**

Consumerism | CATALOG CULTURE

Title: BEST IN SHOW (PG-13)
Warner Bros., 2000

Scripture: Ecclesiastes 5:10-11

Alternate Takes: Contentment (Hebrews 13:5), Dating (Genesis 2:18-24)

START TIME:	11 minutes, 45 seconds
START CUE:	Meg says, "We met at Starbucks."
END TIME:	13 minutes, 30 seconds
END CUE:	Meg says, "Or not."
DURATION:	1 minute, 45 seconds

Overview: Hamilton and Meg recount how they met at adjacent Starbucks, bonded over their shared love of catalogs, and got married.

Illustration: Our society revolves around buying goods and services to the point that some people's entire lives revolve around dreaming about shopping, planning shopping, and actually going shopping. Use this discussion to help break the bonds of consumerism that bind so many young people.

Questions

- Do you know anyone like this—a person who is really into certain stores, brands, or trends? Why is he or she like that?
- What factors make our society so focused on wanting and buying new things?

Read aloud Ecclesiastes 5:10-11.

- Why doesn't getting more stuff bring true satisfaction?
- How can a person find true satisfaction outside of getting more and more stuff?
- What are some consumer attitudes that you need to break, and how can you do that?

Contentment | I WISH I WAS...

Title: BEDAZZLED (PG-13)
20th Century Fox, 2000

Scripture: Philippians 4:10-13

Alternate Take: Spiritual Journey (Romans 5:1-5)

START TIME:	1 hour, 17 minutes, 00 seconds
START CUE:	Elliot enters the devil's office.
END TIME:	1 hour, 18 minutes, 30 seconds
END CUE:	Elliot says, "It's how we get there that really matters."
DURATION:	1 minute, 30 seconds

Overview: Elliot doesn't want any more wishes. He realizes that getting what he wants instantly doesn't bring happiness. He believes it doesn't matter how far someone goes in life; what really matters is the path the person takes to get there.

Illustration: It's hard to be content with life. People always wish for more money, a better body, more friends, and a million other things. Yet when they get those things, they usually still feel empty inside. This scene can help you show teenagers that true contentment comes from resting in the blessings God has already granted his children.

Questions

- What would you change in your life if you had a magic wish? Why?
- Do you think people are generally content with their lives? Why or why not?

Read aloud Philippians 4:10-13.

- Is it really possible to be content when you're going through difficult times? Explain.
- How can you learn to be content in every situation?

Contentment | I WISH I WAS...

Title: BIG (PG)
20th Century Fox, 1988

Scripture: 1 Thessalonians 5:16-18

Alternate Take: Prayer (James 4:2-3)

START TIME:	7 minutes, 30 seconds
START CUE:	Josh sees the coin-operated fortuneteller.
END TIME:	9 minutes, 45 seconds
END CUE:	Josh runs away.
DURATION:	2 minutes, 15 seconds

Overview: Josh, a little kid, wishes he was big at a coin-operated fortunetelling machine.

Illustration: It seems like we're always wanting something different—to be older or younger, smarter or prettier, richer or stronger. Use this clip to encourage teenagers to develop an attitude like Paul's, who learned to be content in all circumstances and discovered lasting joy.

Questions

- **If you could change one thing about your life with a wish, what would it be and why?**
- **What motivates people to crave things they don't have or can't change?** Read aloud 1 Thessalonians 5:16-18.
- **Why is it so difficult to be "joyful always"?**
- **How can you learn to be content in all circumstances like Paul?**

Control | MASTER OF THE UNIVERSE

Title: JURASSIC PARK (PG-13)
Universal Pictures, 1993

Scripture: Luke 12:16-20

Alternate Takes: Illusion (Ezekiel 12:2), Belief (John 20:29)

START TIME:	1 hour, 25 minutes, 15 seconds
START CUE:	Sattler sits at the table.
END TIME:	1 hour, 28 minutes, 15 seconds
END CUE:	Sattler eats some ice cream.
DURATION:	3 minutes

Overview: Hammond describes how people used to watch his flea circus and claim to see the fleas performing. He explains that he wants Jurassic Park to be something real, not an illusion, and promises to make things perfect. Sattler disagrees with Hammond, telling him that he can't control everything.

Illustration: People may attempt to control everything in their lives, but their efforts are futile. Help teenagers see that releasing their lives to God's control will provide them the security they can never achieve through their own power.

Questions

- **What are some things people try to control in life but can't?**
  Read aloud Luke 12:16-20.
- **What makes trying to control life foolish?**
- **What types of things can a human being actually control?**
- **What may be some of the benefits of surrendering control of your life to God?**

Convictions | WALK THIS WAY

Title: DEAD POETS SOCIETY (PG)
Touchstone Pictures, 1989

Scripture: John 17:14-18

Alternate Takes: Peer Pressure (Proverbs 1:10-16), Learning (Psalm 111:10)

START TIME:	1 hour, 3 minutes, 30 seconds
START CUE:	Professor Keating and his class stand in the courtyard.
END TIME:	1 hour, 5 minutes, 45 seconds
END CUE:	A man looks out the window at the class.
DURATION:	2 minutes, 15 seconds

Overview: Professor Keating asks three students to walk around the courtyard. The boys walk around in unison like a marching band. Keating then challenges his students to break free from conformity and think for themselves, following their own unique path.

Illustration: Society calls us to join lock step with its views on faith, social issues, and commerce. God, however, calls us to be in the world but not of it. Many people may think of Christians as mindless marchers, yet we are actually the ones walking free of worldly chains. Use this clip to help students realize that their own unique Christlike walk will draw others to the freedom found on the narrow path to righteousness.

Questions

- **What things and ideas do people "march in unison" for today?**
- **Have you ever compromised your beliefs in order to walk in unison with others? What happened?**
- **Have you ever stuck by your convictions by walking differently from the crowd? What happened?**
  Read aloud John 17:14-18.
- **What does it mean to be in the world but not of the world?**
- **How can a Christian stand firm in his or her convictions?**

Courage | I'LL SHOW YOU!

Title: PEARL HARBOR (PG-13)
Touchstone Pictures, 2001

Scripture: Joshua 1:5-9

Alternate Takes: The Impossible (Luke 18:27), Humility (Luke 18:9-14)

START TIME:	Tape/Disc 2, 00 minutes, 00 seconds
START CUE:	President Roosevelt meets with his cabinet.
END TIME:	Tape/Disc 2, 3 minutes, 00 seconds
END CUE:	President Roosevelt stands.
DURATION:	3 minutes

Overview: The president's advisers tell him that the U.S. military doesn't have the ability to retaliate directly against Japan. President Roosevelt says that victory is never achieved without danger. He explains that he was once strong and proud, but God brought him down into a wheelchair to remind him what humans are. The president then struggles to stand, saying, "Do not tell me it can't be done!"

Illustration: There are countless situations in life that appear impossible. Yet God commands his people to be strong and courageous. We shouldn't look at the world and situations only with our physical eyes, but with a spiritual courage that comes from a deep-rooted faith that the God we serve can accomplish amazing things through our wobbly legs of faith.

Questions
- When have you seen courage displayed?
- How does a person become courageous?

Read aloud Joshua 1:5-9.

- Why should you have courage in every situation?
- What "impossible" areas of life are you facing personally, and how can you confront them with courage?

Dancing | IS THAT LEGAL?

Title: CAN'T BUY ME LOVE (PG-13)
Touchstone Pictures, 1987

Scripture: Psalm 150

Alternate Take: Conformity (Romans 12:1-2)

START TIME:	51 minutes, 45 seconds
START CUE:	Ronald and Patty walk onto the dance floor.
END TIME:	54 minutes, 00 seconds
END CUE:	The entire gym dances like Ronald.
DURATION:	2 minutes, 15 seconds

Overview: Ronald busts out in a crazy dance. People look at him weird, but soon they all start mimicking Ronald because he's popular.

Illustration: No one debates that dancing makes up an important part of teen culture. The opinions fly, however, over the proper how, when, and where of dancing. Use this funny scene to open up some honest dialogue and to provide a spiritual perspective on this issue.

Questions
- Why do people dance?
- Is it possible to dance in a way that pleases God? Explain.

Read aloud Psalm 150.

- What determines whether a dance praises God or not?
- Is it wrong to dance for personal enjoyment? Explain.
- Where is the line between proper and improper dancing, and how can you remain on the right side of the line?

David and Goliath | TAKE YOUR BEST SHOT

Title: KEEPING THE FAITH (PG-13)
Touchstone Pictures, 2000

Scripture: 1 Samuel 17:42-50

Alternate Takes: Idols (1 John 5:20-21),
Pride (Jeremiah 49:16), Trusting God (1 Samuel 17:42-50)

START TIME:	23 minutes, 30 seconds
START CUE:	Jake sees some exercise videos.
END TIME:	24 minutes, 45 seconds
END CUE:	Jake's date says, "Just get my bag."
DURATION:	1 minute, 15 seconds

Overview: Jake's date claims that exercise is her religion and that she has incredible abs. She tells Jake to punch her in the stomach, but he refuses. She keeps nagging him until he gives in. When he punches her, she collapses to the floor.

Illustration: In this case, "pride goeth before collapse"! It seems as if every time we become supremely confident in our own abilities, something comes along to slap us off our high horse. Use this discussion to encourage your youth to rely on God alone as David did, instead of placing prideful confidence in their own strength and abilities as Goliath did.

Questions

- **Why did the woman place so much confidence in her muscles?**
  Read aloud 1 Samuel 17:42-50.
- **What gave Goliath confidence? What gave David confidence?**
- **Do you approach life's obstacles more like David or Goliath? Explain.**
- **In which areas of your life do you trust your own abilities instead of trusting God?**
- **How can you learn to place your faith in God instead of yourself?**

Denying Christ | JESUS WHO?

Title: THE OTHERS (PG-13)
Dimension Films, 2001

Scripture: Matthew 10:32-33

Alternate Takes: The Afterlife (Hebrews 9:27-28),
Integrity (Daniel 6:3-5), Lies (Proverbs 19:9)

START TIME:	14 minutes, 30 seconds
START CUE:	The family sits around the table.
END TIME:	17 minutes, 00 seconds
END CUE:	The kids nod their heads yes.
DURATION:	2 minutes, 30 seconds

Overview: Nicholas reads about martyrs who wouldn't deny Christ. The kids think that's dumb; they think it would've been smarter for the martyrs to save their lives simply by denying Jesus with their lips while still believing in their hearts. Grace explains that though they would save their lives on earth, God would know for eternity that they had denied him.

Illustration: Many people claim allegiance to or ignorance of Christ as the situation suits them. Yet the Bible clearly states that those who deny him before men will find themselves disowned in the afterlife. Use this discussion to challenge your students to keep the cross on their shoulders at all times.

Questions
- **Do you agree with the children or the mother? Why?**
  Read aloud Matthew 10:32-33.
- **What are some ways that people disown Jesus?**
- **How can God reject people if he's full of forgiveness and love?**
- **How can you be more public in acknowledging Jesus in your life?**

The Devil | IS THAT A PITCHFORK?

Title: BEDAZZLED (PG-13)
20th Century Fox, 2000

Scripture: Revelation 12:7-9

Alternate Take: Temptation (Matthew 4:1-11)

START TIME:	13 minutes, 15 seconds
START CUE:	Elliot asks, "Who are you?"
END TIME:	16 minutes, 00 seconds
END CUE:	The devil asks, "How about respected? How about feared?"
DURATION:	2 minutes, 45 seconds

Overview: Elliot meets a gorgeous woman who claims to be the devil. Elliot doesn't believe her until she performs several devilish miracles to prove it. She claims to only want Elliot to be happy by making him liked, loved, respected, and even feared.

Themes D-F

Humor

37

Illustration: The devil may not be omnipotent, but he knows how to hit our soft spots unexpectedly. Unfortunately, many have bought into a caricature of our enemy (viewing him as a red cartoon guy with a pitchfork) instead of remaining wary of the devourer who seeks our destruction. Use this scene to discuss who the devil really is and how to guard against him.

Questions
- **What do you know about the devil?**
- **What reasons do people have for not believing in the devil?**
  Read aloud Revelation 12:7-9.
- **Why should we be wary of the devil if God is going to win in the end?**
- **How can you guard yourself against the devil's schemes?**

The Disabled | I'M SPECIAL

Title: THE MIGHTY (PG-13)
Miramax Films, 1998

Scripture: Leviticus 19:14-15
Alternate Take: Kindness (Ephesians 4:32–5:2)

START TIME:	9 minutes, 30 seconds
START CUE:	A basketball goes through the hoop.
END TIME:	11 minutes, 00 seconds
END CUE:	Kevin throws the ball at Max and helps himself up.
DURATION:	1 minute, 30 seconds

Overview: Blade rolls a basketball across the gym so it knocks Kevin, a disabled boy, off his feet. Max gets blamed for the prank and goes over to help Kevin get up, but Kevin doesn't accept the help.

Illustration: God loves all of his creation equally and asks that we pay special attention to the weak, defenseless, and disabled in society. Use this poignant scene to explore ways teenagers in your ministry can show the love of God to those who are disabled.

Questions
- **How do you usually react towards people with disabilities?**
- **Why do people treat the disabled poorly?**
  Read aloud Leviticus 19:14-15.
- **How does helping the disabled honor God?**
- **What are some ways you can reach out to the disabled people in our community?**

Title: MEET THE PARENTS (PG-13)
Universal Pictures, 2000

Scripture: Luke 6:40
Alternate Takes: Talents (Colossians 3:23-24),
Creativity (Exodus 35:30-33)

START TIME:	55 minutes, 30 seconds
START CUE:	They enter the wood shop.
END TIME:	56 minutes, 15 seconds
END CUE:	Kevin says, "You're in good company."
DURATION:	45 seconds

Overview: Kevin displays his impressive carpentry work. He explains that he got into it because he wanted to follow in Jesus' footsteps.

Illustration: While Kevin's goal is admirable, there are probably better ways to emulate Christ than carpentry. Jesus clearly wants his children to become disciples, but what exactly that means can be confusing to people. Since we can't walk around physically following Jesus, use this clip to help teenagers understand what it really means to live as a dedicated disciple.

Questions
- **What does it mean to be a disciple of Jesus?**
  Read aloud Luke 6:40.
- **How can a human being possibly become like Jesus?**
- **How should discipleship affect every area of your life?**
- **What are some practical ways to become a better disciple of Jesus?**

Title: CHARLIE'S ANGELS (PG-13)
Columbia Pictures, 2000

Scripture: Matthew 6:31-34
Alternate Takes: Prayer (Matthew 6:5-6),
Preparation (2 Timothy 4:1-8)

START TIME:	1 hour, 12 minutes, 30 seconds
START CUE:	Natalie finds Bosley.
END TIME:	1 hour, 13 minutes, 30 seconds
END CUE:	Natalie gets back on the phone.
DURATION:	1 minute

Overview: Natalie gets a phone call while she's rescuing Bosley. She talks with Pete, but gets distracted when some men attack her. She quickly defeats her assailants and then returns to the phone conversation.

Illustration: There are a million and one things that distract us from the important things in life. It's especially hard to focus on the spiritual things (prayer and Bible study, for example) with the world always pressing in. Use this scene to suggest ways teenagers can prioritize the important activities in life and ignore the distractions.

Questions

- **What are some things that distract you from God?**
- **Why is it easy to get distracted from spiritual things?**
  Read aloud Matthew 6:31-34.
- **What things are we supposed to pay attention to?**
- **How does focusing on spiritual things first help you accomplish all the rest of your duties?**
- **What are some practical ways to filter out distractions?**

Doubts | IT'S LEAKING!

Title: U-571 (PG-13)
Universal Pictures, 2000

Scripture: James 1:2-6

Alternate Takes: Faith (Isaiah 31:1-3),
Peter Walking on Water (Matthew 14:25-32)

START TIME:	21 minutes, 15 seconds
START CUE:	Tyler says, "Bridge hatch shut."
END TIME:	23 minutes, 45 seconds
END CUE:	Dahlgren says, "She's old, but she'll hold."
DURATION:	2 minutes, 30 seconds

Overview: The submarine dives under water. Drips turn to leaks as the sub plunges deeper. Dahlgren explains the depth and pressure the sub can withstand and assures Hirsch and Coonan not to worry.

Illustration: The adventure really takes off once you climb inside the submarine of faith. Though it takes a lot for someone to completely abandon ship, leaks in our assurance are certain to spring up along the journey. Use this scene to encourage your young people in the face of their doubts, helping them find peace even when they fear they might sink.

Questions

- **What doubts about God have "leaked" into your faith? Why?**
  Read aloud James 1:2-6.
- **Is doubting a sin? Why or why not?**
- **Where can a person turn for reassurance in times of doubt?**
- **How can a person address his or her doubts while still maintaining a strong faith?**

Dysfunctional Families | I'M DIFFERENT

Title: THE MIGHTY (PG-13)
Miramax Films, 1998

Scripture: Ezekiel 18:1-9

Alternate Take: Deeds (Titus 1:16)

START TIME:	40 minutes, 30 seconds
START CUE:	Max sits on a bench.
END TIME:	41 minutes, 45 seconds
END CUE:	Max and Kevin look out over the city.
DURATION:	1 minute, 15 seconds

Overview: Max is upset because his father was a terrible criminal. Kevin tells Max how he was abandoned by his own dad but that doesn't define Kevin as a person. He encourages Max and tells him that knights prove their worthiness by their deeds and don't have to follow in their fathers' footsteps.

Illustration: Many times we feel doomed to repeat the mistakes of our parents, whether we want to or not. Thankfully, the redeeming power of Christ breaks this cycle of sin and helps us take a righteous path. Use this scene to help teenagers realize that their futures need not be determined by the dysfunctions in their families.

Questions

- **Why do people often become like their parents?**
- **Do you want to be like your parents? Why or why not?**
  Read aloud Ezekiel 18:1-9.

- What commands does God give for avoiding consequences for your parents' poor habits?
- In which area of your life do you want to be different from your parents, and how can you achieve that?

Easter | HE'S ALIVE!

Title: E.T. THE EXTRA-TERRESTRIAL (PG)
Universal Pictures, 1982

Scripture: Luke 18:31-33

Alternate Takes: Death (Philippians 1:19-22), The Afterlife (Romans 8:9-11)

START TIME:	1 hour, 32 minutes, 30 seconds
START CUE:	Elliot says, "Look at what they've done to you."
END TIME:	1 hour, 35 minutes, 30 seconds
END CUE:	Elliot tells Michael, "He's alive!"
DURATION:	3 minutes

Overview: While E.T. lies dead in a laboratory casket, Elliot mourns over his body. Yet, as Elliot professes his love for E.T., the extra-terrestrial suddenly returns to life! Elliot is shocked and overjoyed at the resurrection.

Illustration: Jesus died and rose again to the joy of all those who love and believe in him. This beloved scene provides a modern illustration of the experience of the disciples when they first proclaimed, "He has risen!"

Questions
- **How does this scene symbolize the life of Jesus?**
  Read aloud Luke 18:31-33.
- **Why did Jesus have to die and rise again?**
- **How does Jesus' death and resurrection separate Christianity from every other religion?**
- **How can you make Easter a more meaningful celebration this year?**

Enthusiasm | GOT ANY?

Title: LEGALLY BLONDE (PG-13)
MGM, 2001

Scripture: Titus 2:11-14
Alternate Take: Faith (Isaiah 31:1)

START TIME:	1 hour, 29 minutes, 00 seconds
START CUE:	Elle takes the podium.
END TIME:	1 hour, 30 minutes, 30 seconds
END CUE:	The audience claps and cheers.
DURATION:	1 minute, 30 seconds

Overview: Elle gives the graduation speech. She quotes Aristotle, who said that the law is reason free from passion. Elle disagrees because she believes passion is the key ingredient to law and life.

Illustration: People are enthusiastic about their true loves. A favorite sports team, one's family, favorite shoes, or anything that consumes one's thoughts and energy shows where that person's true dedication lies. Use this clip to encourage your students to be passionate in faith and enthusiastic for doing good.

Questions
- **What are some things you are passionate and enthusiastic about?**
  Read aloud Titus 2:11-14.
- **What does God want us to be enthusiastic about?**
- **Can you love God without being excited about it? Explain.**
- **How can you show passion for God by "doing good" regularly?**

The Environment | WHO'S IN CHARGE?

Title: DR. DOLITTLE 2 (PG)
20th Century Fox, 2001

Scripture: Deuteronomy 20:19-20
Alternate Takes: Helping Others (Proverbs 14:31), Animals (Psalm 8)

START TIME:	17 minutes, 00 seconds
START CUE:	Dr. Dolittle walks into the clearing and says, "Hello."
END TIME:	19 minutes, 00 seconds
END CUE:	The squirrel says, "Everything…gone."
DURATION:	2 minutes

Overview: Dr. Dolittle meets the beaver and his crew. He asks for Dr. Dolittle's help in stopping the humans from cutting down the forest. The doctor refuses to help until he sees what the loggers are doing. The animals show him the devastation—the entire forest is cut down.

Illustration: God gave humanity stewardship of the earth. This means different things to different people. Some see it as a license to use and abuse all natural resources, while others take another extreme—protecting the environment as if they were subservient to it. Use this discussion to help students discern what their responsibility is in protecting God's creation without elevating it to "god status."

Questions

- **How do you feel about environmental issues?**
  Read aloud Deuteronomy 20:19-20.

- **In this passage, why do you think God cares if people cut down fruit trees?**

- **How can a Christian determine what are proper and improper uses of environmental resources?**

- **What is a Christian's responsibility toward the environment?**

Euthanasia | YOU CAN'T CHOOSE

Title: THE LORD OF THE RINGS:
THE FELLOWSHIP OF THE RING (PG-13)
New Line Cinema, 2001

Scripture: Ecclesiastes 8:8

Alternate Take: Pity (Proverbs 14:21)

START TIME:	1 hour, 49 minutes, 15 seconds
START CUE:	Frodo turns and spots Gollum.
END TIME:	1 hour, 50 minutes, 45 seconds
END CUE:	Frodo sits next to Gandalf.
DURATION:	1 minute, 30 seconds

Overview: Frodo tells Gandalf he wishes his uncle Bilbo had killed Gollum when he had the chance. Gandalf responds by scolding Frodo, reminding him that he doesn't have the right to deal out death and judgement.

Illustration: Many people believe that we can decide who should live or die. Euthanasia is an issue that can seem very confusing because it's often motivated by feelings of compassion. Yet, euthanasia ultimately usurps God's role and robs people of their most precious gift—life. Use this clip to discuss the slippery moral slope involved in assisted suicide.

Questions

- Why shouldn't a person have the right to decide who lives and dies?
- What are the arguments for euthanasia (assisted suicide)? What are the arguments against it?

Read aloud Ecclesiastes 8:8.

- What does this passage have to say that could be applied to the topic of assisted suicide?
- Why doesn't God want us to kill someone who's in pain?
- How can a Christian help someone who is in physical, mental, or emotional pain?

Evil | LOOK IN MY HEART

Title: X-MEN (PG-13)
20th Century Fox, 2000

Scripture: James 1:13-16

Alternate Takes: The Israelites (1 Kings 8:53), Injustice (Psalm 82:1-4), Racism (Colossians 3:9-11)

START TIME:	1 minute, 15 seconds
START CUE:	Muddy feet walk in the rain.
END TIME:	4 minutes, 15 seconds
END CUE:	A soldier looks at the bent gates.
DURATION:	3 minutes

Overview: Jews are filed into a concentration camp set up by the Nazis. The soldiers separate a young Jewish boy from his family. The boy yells and tries to reach his family, but the Nazis grab him and only stop him after knocking him unconscious.

Illustration: The Holocaust is but one terrible event that exemplifies man's basic wickedness and capability for great evil. Start a discussion that will explore the depths of the human heart and help your teenagers understand not only where evil springs from but how to fight against it.

Questions

- What are some acts of evil that have occurred in history or in recent times?
- Do you believe humans are basically good or basically evil? Explain.

Read aloud James 1:13-16.

- Why do people often blame God instead of humans for evil in the world?
- How does understanding the source of evil change your view of the world?

Expectations | YOU WERE EXPECTING A PRINCE?

Title: SHREK (PG)
DreamWorks SKG, 2001

Scripture: Genesis 12:1-3

Alternate Takes: Road to Emmaus (Luke 24:13-21),
Appearances (John 7:24), True Love (1 Corinthians 13)

START TIME:	40 minutes, 15 seconds
START CUE:	Fiona slides down the mountain.
END TIME:	43 minutes, 15 seconds
END CUE:	Fiona says, "I'll be waiting for him right here."
DURATION:	3 minutes

Overview: Fiona thanks Shrek and asks to see his face since she believes it's destiny for him to be her true love. Shrek and Donkey laugh hysterically. Shrek removes his helmet to reveal he's an ogre. She gets upset because he's supposed to be a prince!

Illustration: Everyone has expectations for how things are gonna go in life, and those expectations are rarely met. Use this funny scene to help your teenagers understand the difference between looking forward to the future and planning out exactly how they'd like the future to unfold.

Questions

- **Do things ever happen as you expect them? Why or why not?**
  Read aloud Genesis 12:1-3.
- **How do you think Abram expected God to fulfill his promise?**
- **How did God actually fulfill the promise?**
- **Why does God often do things in ways we don't expect?**
- **How can you plan for the future without having detailed expectations of God?**

Facades | IT'S NOT HALLOWEEN

Title: JURASSIC PARK III (PG-13)
Universal Pictures, 2001

Scripture: Leviticus 19:11

Alternate Takes: Lies (Colossians 3:9-10), Pride (Galatians 6:3-4)

START TIME:	30 minutes, 45 seconds
START CUE:	Billy and Dr. Grant watch Mr. Kirby.
END TIME:	32 minutes, 00 seconds
END CUE:	Mr. Udesky says, "Never can tell about people."
DURATION:	1 minute, 15 seconds

Overview: Billy and Dr. Grant question Mr. Kirby about his alleged mountain climbing skills. Mr. Kirby admits he's never climbed and there is no such thing as Kirby Enterprises. The truth is he runs a paint and tile company. Mr. Udesky also admits he's just a booking agent, not a mercenary.

Illustration: It's easy to talk the talk, but walking a genuine walk separates the real deal from the posers. Whether people are trying to impress others or are simply pretending, their facades will eventually crack. Use this scene to help teenagers understand that God knows exactly who we are and wants us to be honest about ourselves with others.

Questions
- **What motivates a person to pretend to be something he or she isn't?**
- **How do facades hurt others? hurt the people who use them?**
  Read aloud Leviticus 19:11.
- **Why does God lump dealing falsely together with stealing?**
- **How do you see others living falsely?**
- **Are there any facades in your life, and if so, how can you remove them?**

Faith | I KNOW IT WHEN I SEE IT

Title: KEEPING THE FAITH (PG-13)
Touchstone Pictures, 2000

Scripture: Hebrews 11
Alternate Take: Religion (Mark 7:1-8)

START TIME:	12 minutes, 45 seconds
START CUE:	Brian says, "The truth is..."
END TIME:	13 minutes, 45 seconds
END CUE:	Brian says, "Let us pray."
DURATION:	1 minute

Overview: Brian, a Catholic priest, explains to his congregation the difference between faith and religion. He explains that faith is a hunch and that hunch is God. Connecting to that hunch is an act of faith.

Illustration: Faith is that intangible, easy-to-identify, but hard to describe kernel of what it means to follow Jesus Christ. Expand upon Brian's simple explanation of faith to get to the heart of what it actually looks like in real life and how people can place assurance in something they can't see.

Questions

- **What gives you confidence that your faith is real?**
- **How does your faith help you feel connected to God?**
  Read aloud Hebrews 11.
- **Can you have faith like these men and women? Explain.**
- **How can you build up your faith?**

Faith Journey | WHAT I'M TRYING TO SAY IS...

Title: BATMAN (PG-13)
Warner Bros., 1989

Scripture: Mark 8:34-38

Alternate Takes: Sharing Faith (2 Corinthians 4:13-15), Facades (Leviticus 19:11)

START TIME:	1 hour, 19 minutes, 15 seconds
START CUE:	Vicki falls into the chair.
END TIME:	1 hour, 21 minutes, 00 seconds
END CUE:	Vicki leaves Bruce to answer the door.
DURATION:	1 minute, 45 seconds

Overview: Bruce struggles to reveal to Vicki that he's Batman without actually coming out and saying it, explaining instead how some people have different sides to their personalities.

Illustration: Sometimes it's hard to come right out and talk about our relationship with Christ. Whether we think the name *Jesus* will offend someone or the person won't understand or will reject us doesn't matter. There's no excuse for candy-coating your testimony, so challenge your youth to get their story straight and share it with confidence.

Questions

- **Have you ever been embarrassed about telling a person you were a Christian? If so, why and what happened?**
  Read aloud Mark 8:34-38.
- **Why would a person deny Christ before other people?**

- How exactly would you share the story of your Christian faith journey with someone?
- How does knowing your personal faith story make it easier to share with others?

Faith's Foundation | KEEP YOUR GRIP

Title: MISSION: IMPOSSIBLE II (PG-13)
Paramount Pictures, 2000

Scripture: Matthew 7:21-27

Alternate Take: Self-Reliance (Obadiah 2-4)

START TIME:	6 minutes, 00 seconds
START CUE:	Ethan Hunt rock climbs.
END TIME:	8 minutes, 00 seconds
END CUE:	Ethan Hunt hangs from the mountain.
DURATION:	2 minutes

Overview: Ethan Hunt climbs the face of a towering mountain without a rope, partner, or net. He slips and nearly plummets to his death, saving his life by clinging to a rock.

Illustration: We've got to stay connected to the rock of Jesus Christ, clinging desperately to his solid foundation in order to make it in this wacky world. Though we might slip at times, we'll never fall far if we hold tight to the one true Rock.

Questions

- What types of "foundations" do people build their lives upon? Read aloud Matthew 7:21-27.
- How can a person build a foundation on rock in his or her life?
- Why does the Bible use "rock" imagery when referring to God?
- What do you need to do to stay focused on God as your foundation in life?

Family | GET ME OUTTA HERE

Title: HOME ALONE (PG)
20th Century Fox, 1990

Scripture: Proverbs 11:29

Alternate Take: Punishment (Hebrews 12:5-11)

START TIME:	11 minutes, 30 seconds
START CUE:	Kevin and his mom walk upstairs.
END TIME:	12 minutes, 45 seconds
END CUE:	Mom closes the door.
DURATION:	1 minute, 15 seconds

Overview: Kevin is sent to the third floor as punishment. He says, "I hope I never see any of you jerks again!"

Illustration: Families should be a source of love and comfort, but they often cause a good deal of strife, too. God put you in your family for a reason, and he's there to help you—whether your family tree is bearing fruit or wilting.

Questions
- Have you ever wished you were in a different family? Why or why not?
- What do you like about your family? What do you dislike about your family? Read aloud Proverbs 11:29.
- Why does trouble at home cause a whirlwind?
- What obligation do you have to your family, even if they don't treat you well?
- How can you serve your family this week?

Fasting | MY STOMACH'S GROWLING

Title: SISTER ACT (PG)
Touchstone Pictures, 1992

Scripture: Ezra 8:21-23

Alternate Takes: Contentment (Philippians 4:10-13), Obedience (Deuteronomy 26:16-17)

START TIME:	24 minutes, 30 seconds
START CUE:	The nuns sit.
END TIME:	25 minutes, 45 seconds
END CUE:	Sister Mary Clarence looks down at the empty spot in front of her.
DURATION:	1 minute, 15 seconds

Overview: Sister Mary Clarence complains about the terrible food at the abbey. The mother superior announces that Mary Clarence will have a ritual fast. Mary Clarence suddenly wants the food, but it's taken away from her.

Illustration: Fasting doesn't get a lot of press these days, but it's an important spiritual discipline practiced throughout Scripture. Start on a light note with this scene, then explore the spiritual purpose and benefits of fasting.

Questions

- Have you ever fasted? Why or why not?
  Read aloud Ezra 8:21-23.
- What reason did Ezra have to fast? What are some other reasons Christians fast?
- How can fasting bring a person closer to God?
- What reasons might people have for not fasting?
- How can you make fasting a regular part of your spiritual walk?

Fear | I'M PHOBIC

Title: BANDITS (PG-13)
MGM, 2001

Scripture: Psalm 23

Alternate Take: Confession (Joshua 7:19-21)

START TIME:	1 hour, 14 minutes, 15 seconds
START CUE:	Terry says, "I have food allergies."
END TIME:	1 hour, 15 minutes, 15 seconds
END CUE:	Terry says, "I never thought of it that way."
DURATION:	1 minute

Overview: Terry lists off his numerous phobias: antiques, black and white movies, getting smaller, and so on.

Illustration: Fear can paralyze a person, but God's children have his promise of protection. Remind your young people they have nothing to fear with God as their shield.

Questions

- What are some other phobias you've heard of?
- What is your greatest fear in life?
  Read aloud Psalm 23.
- Why should God's children live free of fear?
- How can you bring the peace of God into your life when you feel fear creeping up on you?

Forgiveness | THERE'S NO CHOICE

Title: THE MAN IN THE MOON (PG-13)
MGM, 1991

Scripture: Matthew 18:23-35

Alternate Take: Compassion (1 John 3:16-18)

START TIME:	1 hour, 29 minutes, 45 seconds
START CUE:	Dani and her dad fish.
END TIME:	1 hour, 31 minutes, 30 seconds
END CUE:	Dani thinks about what her dad said.
DURATION:	1 minute, 45 seconds

Overview: Dani feels as if she can't forgive her sister for dating the boy she loved. Dad tells Dani she has a right to feel hurt, but if she can't see her sister's pain, she's completely useless; her sister is hurting and needs her.

Illustration: It's hard to forgive others when we've been wronged, but we don't have a choice in the matter. God has forgiven us far more than we'll ever be asked to forgive. Use this discussion to encourage your young people to forgive those around them freely just as Christ has forgiven them.

Questions

- **What is something that's hard for you to forgive?**
  Read aloud Matthew 18:23-35.
- **Why do we hold grudges against others when God has forgiven us so much?**
- **Does forgiveness involve forgetting too? Explain.**
- **How do you know when you've truly forgiven someone?**
- **Who do you need to forgive in your life and how can you do that?**

The Future | NO PROMISES HERE

Title: CAST AWAY (PG-13)
20th Century Fox, 2000

Scripture: Luke 12:16-23

Alternate Takes: The Magi (Matthew 2:1-12),
Marriage (Matthew 19:4-6)

START TIME:	17 minutes, 45 seconds
START CUE:	The car stops at the airport.
END TIME:	20 minutes, 45 seconds
END CUE:	Chuck says, "I'll be right back."
DURATION:	3 minutes

Overview: Chuck and Kelly exchange Christmas gifts before he leaves. Finally, Chuck proposes marriage, gives her an engagement ring, and leaves on a business trip.

Illustration: Everyone knows Chuck didn't make it right back. Though God probably won't strand you on a desert island to teach you a lesson, he does warn us about the folly of relying on our own plans. Encourage teenagers to look to the future with a balanced perspective, knowing that God might redirect their course.

Questions

- **What plans do you have for the future?**
- **How does God fit into or influence your future plans?**
  Read aloud Luke 12:16-23.
- **How can a person look to the future without anxiety?**
- **How can you plan for the future while being open to God changing those plans?**

Generosity | YOU GET...A NEW CAR!

Title: PAY IT FORWARD (PG-13)
Warner Bros., 2000

Scripture: Luke 10:30-37
Alternate Takes: Providence (Job 5:9-11),
Possessions (1 John 2:15-17)

START TIME:	2 minutes, 15 seconds
START CUE:	Chris' car gets smashed.
END TIME:	4 minutes, 30 seconds
END CUE:	The stranger leaves Chris with the Jaguar.
DURATION:	2 minutes, 15 seconds

Overview: Chris Chandler watches his vintage Mustang get totaled by a fleeing criminal. He stands stranded in the rain when a complete stranger shows up and gives Chandler a brand new Jaguar. Chandler thinks the man's generosity is insane. No one just gives away a brand new Jaguar!

Illustration: Few people believe in the existence of no-strings-attached generosity. Yet Christians should be *known* for their supernatural ability to minister to immediate needs. Use this discussion to show teenagers that by giving our time and resources generously to desperate people, the love of Christ will permeate an unbelieving world.

Questions
- **Have you ever helped a stranger in need? What happened?**
- **Are Christians known for their generosity? Why or why not?**
  Read aloud Luke 10:30-37.
- **How would being a "good Samaritan" to others change the world?**
- **How can you learn to be more aware of the needs around you?**
- **How can you be more generous with your time and resources in the future?**

Gifts and Offerings | GIVE IT ALL?!

Title: RAT RACE (PG-13)
Paramount Pictures, 2001

Scripture: 2 Corinthians 9:5-7
Alternate Takes: Generosity (1 John 3:16-18),
The Less Fortunate (Exodus 22:21-27)

START TIME:	1 hour, 38 minutes, 30 seconds
START CUE:	The old man says, "We work for Feed the Earth."
END TIME:	1 hour, 41 minutes, 30 seconds
END CUE:	Duane gives his money.
DURATION:	3 minutes

Overview: The racers don't want to donate their money to charity, but the starving children who thank them change their hearts, and one by one the racers drop their winnings into the bag. Duane still hangs on, but his brother convinces him to give his money away.

Illustration: God loves a cheerful giver, and there are lots of people in need who would be happy to receive your charitable contributions. Challenge your youth to look at their spending habits and find ways to generously and cheerfully bless others with their abundance.

Questions
- **What are some worthy causes you think people should support with their money?**
- **What prevents you from giving more of your time and money to the causes and people you believe in?**

Read aloud 2 Corinthians 9:5-7.
- **What should be a person's motivation for giving gifts and offerings?**
- **How can a person learn to become cheerful when giving?**

Giving | I'M SACRIFICING HERE!

Title: RETURN TO ME (PG)
  MGM, 2000

Scripture: Matthew 6:1-4
Alternate Take: Humility (Luke 1:49-55)

START TIME:	9 minutes, 45 seconds
START CUE:	Mr. Bennington says, "Bob!"
END TIME:	11 minutes, 30 seconds
END CUE:	Charlie says, "A mural."
DURATION:	1 minute, 45 seconds

Overview: Mr. Bennington keeps talking about his sizable "anonymous" donation to the zoo. Bob avoids further conversation by dragging Charlie in and claiming he's going to put Mr. Bennington's picture up in the monkey house.

Illustration: God wants us to join in his work by quietly giving our money back to him. Use this scene to challenge those in your ministry to cheerfully give their money to the kingdom of God without expecting an earthly return on their investment.

Questions
- **What is the purpose of giving money to the church?**
- **What reasons do people have for not giving money?**
  Read aloud Matthew 6:1-4.
- **Why should we give our money in secret?**
- **What are the benefits of joyfully giving money to the church?**

God's Character | THAT'S NOT LIKE YOU

Title: STAR TREK V: THE FINAL FRONTIER (PG)
  Paramount Pictures, 1989

Scripture: Psalm 31:1-8
Alternate Take: Questioning God (Jeremiah 12:1-2)

START TIME:	1 hour, 28 minutes, 00 seconds
START CUE:	God says, "It is I."
END TIME:	1 hour, 30 minutes, 30 seconds
END CUE:	"…a vision you created."
DURATION:	2 minutes, 30 seconds

Overview: Sybok offers "God" their starship so they can carry his wisdom past the barrier and throughout the universe. Kirk doesn't buy it and asks why God would need a ship. "God" answers his doubts by shooting him with lightning. McCoy then asserts that he can't believe in a god who inflicts pain for his own pleasure.

Illustration: There are lots of opinions swirling around about who God is and what God does or doesn't do. Most of these people don't really know God though. They may know one of his attributes but not the complex omnipotent being that's described in the Bible. Use this movie illustration to launch into an exploration of God's multifaceted character.

Questions

- **How can a person know God well enough to recognize him?**
  Read aloud Psalm 31:1-8.
- **What are some of the attributes of God mentioned here? What are some other attributes that aren't mentioned here?**
- **What are some common misperceptions about God's character?**
- **How can you improve your knowledge of God's character and how will that help your relationship with him?**

God's Love | HE KNOWS MY NAME!

Title: X-MEN (PG-13)
20th Century Fox, 2000

Scripture: Romans 8:38-39

Alternate Takes: Omniscience (Daniel 2:20-22),
God's Chosen (Ephesians 1:3-6)

START TIME:	45 minutes, 45 seconds
START CUE:	Professor Xavier approaches a machine.
END TIME:	47 minutes, 45 seconds
END CUE:	Professor Xavier locates Rogue and says, "She's at the train station."
DURATION:	2 minutes

Overview: Professor Xavier uses a machine that enhances his telekinetic abilities, to locate Rogue's unique brain waves from the billions that clog the world. He hooks himself up to the machine and pinpoints the missing girl among the multitudes, concerned about her safety.

Illustration: The thought of the mighty God of the universe knowing and caring for us personally seems too good to be true! Yet, he *does* love us intimately and can pick us out of the crowd immediately, even when we try to hide from him. This clip isn't meant to threaten teenagers that "he's always watching" but instead to reinforce the idea that God loves them passionately.

Questions

- **Have you ever gotten lost or separated from your friends? How did you feel?** Read aloud Romans 8:38-39.
- **Why might someone feel separated from God even though his love is constant?**
- **Why does God love people even though we constantly screw up?**
- **How can God's love free you from fear and doubt?**

God's Presence | COULD YOU SPEAK UP?

Title: BATMAN (PG-13)
Warner Bros., 1989

Scripture: Isaiah 43:1-7
Alternate Takes: Prayer (Hebrews 11:6), Community (Acts 2:41-47)

START TIME:	31 minutes, 00 seconds
START CUE:	The front gates close.
END TIME:	32 minutes, 30 seconds
END CUE:	Bruce and Vicki exit.
DURATION:	1 minute, 30 seconds

Overview: Bruce and Vicki sit at opposite ends of an extremely long dining room table eating dinner. They try to eat and converse unsuccessfully because of the wide distance between them. Vicki asks if they can eat together somewhere else.

Illustration: Sometimes it can feel as if God is a million miles away. We need to remember that God hasn't left us but something else might be creating the distance between us and our Father. Use this discussion to help participants find ways to create greater intimacy with God and to identify obstacles that might stand in the way of their efforts to develop a deeper relationship.

Questions

- **When have you felt the farthest from God's presence?**
- **When do you feel closest to God?**
  Read aloud Isaiah 43:1-7.
- **If God promises to always be there, why does his presence sometimes seem to move closer or farther away?**
- **How can we re-establish intimacy with God even when he seems far away?**

God's Wisdom | YOU EXPECT US TO BELIEVE THAT?

Title: STARGATE (PG-13)
  MGM, 1994

Scripture: 1 Corinthians 1:25-31
Alternate Takes: Sharing Faith (Acts 17:1-9),
Tongues (1 Corinthians 14:26-33)

START TIME:	5 minutes, 00 seconds
START CUE:	Text appears that reads "Present Day."
END TIME:	6 minutes, 45 seconds
END CUE:	Daniel asks, "Is there a lunch or something?"
DURATION:	1 minute, 45 seconds

Overview: Daniel explains his controversial belief that the pyramids were not built during the reign of the Pharaohs. His colleagues scoff at him and leave the lecture hall.

Illustration: This is how people often react to God, his Word, and his wisdom. The truth often sounds ridiculous to those who don't believe in Christ, but that doesn't make it any less true. This discussion will help students build up their faith in God's wisdom, even when it appears ludicrous to others.

Questions

- **What Bible teachings sounded ridiculous the first time you heard them?**
- **What happened to make your opinion and beliefs change?**
  Read aloud 1 Corinthians 1:25-31.
- **Why isn't God's truth clear to everyone immediately?**
- **How can you help people understand the importance of spiritual issues they think are foolish?**

The Good Samaritan | A LITTLE HELP HERE!

Humor

Title: SHANGHAI NOON (PG-13)
Touchstone Pictures, 2000

Scripture: Luke 10:25-37

Alternate Takes: Forgiveness (Luke 6:27-36),
Friends (Proverbs 12:26)

START TIME:	18 minutes, 15 seconds
START CUE:	Roy screams, buried in the sand.
END TIME:	20 minutes, 15 seconds
END CUE:	Chon leaves Roy.
DURATION:	2 minutes

Overview: Roy is buried to his neck in the sand. Chon finds him but refuses to help, walking away as if he didn't see anything.

Illustration: While it'd be hard to ignore someone in Roy's position, we don't always succeed at being "good Samaritans" 100 percent of the time. Challenge those involved in your ministry to exhibit Christ through their actions by striving to help *all* of the neighbors they pass by.

Questions
- **What types of needy people get ignored every day?**
- **How do you typically react when you see these people?**
  Read aloud Luke 10:25-37.
- **What prevents people from helping others in need?**
- **Who do you need to start helping, and how can you do that?**

Gossip | WELL, I HEARD...

Drama

Title: THE SPITFIRE GRILL (PG-13)
Columbia Pictures, 1996

Scripture: Proverbs 16:27-28

Alternate Take: Judging (John 7:24)

START TIME:	11 minutes, 00 seconds
START CUE:	Percy approaches customers with coffee.
END TIME:	12 minutes, 15 seconds
END CUE:	Percy exits.
DURATION:	1 minute, 15 seconds

Overview: Everyone in the grill is murmuring about Percy—who she is, where she's from, why she's there—but no one will talk directly to her. Eventually, Percy shouts out to Hannah, "Did I forget to mention I've been in prison?" to cut their gossip short.

Illustration: Gossip is often the overlooked sin. Few people want to give it up because it's so much *fun.* Use this clip to help students understand that God detests this destructive and hurtful habit and calls his children to speak only love and encouragement, not venomous gossip.

Questions
- **Why do people like to gossip?**
  Read aloud Proverbs 16:27-28.
- **Why does God hate something that appears so innocent?**
- **What are some of the results of indulging in gossip?**
- **How can you refrain from participating in gossip?**

Grace | I'M BEGGING YOU

Title: THE HOUSE OF MIRTH (PG)
Sony Pictures Classics, 2000

Scripture: Isaiah 55:6-7

Alternate Takes: Gambling (Luke 16:1-2), Peer Pressure (Proverbs 12:26), Disgrace (Jeremiah 3:25)

START TIME:	48 minutes, 45 seconds
START CUE:	Lily approaches Aunt Julia.
END TIME:	51 minutes, 45 seconds
END CUE:	Lily exits.
DURATION:	3 minutes

Overview: Lily confesses her gambling debts and her foolishness in bending to peer pressure. Lily begs for help in avoiding disgrace, but Aunt Julia refuses.

Illustration: There are times in life where we've blown it royally. Thankfully, God's grace flows even when human "compassion" lets us down. Help teenagers see that God always extends grace to those who humbly repent.

Questions
- **Do you think Aunt Julia did the right thing? Why or why not?**
- **Has anyone ever shown you grace when you didn't deserve it? If so, what happened?**
  Read aloud Isaiah 55:6-7.

- Why does God promise to show us grace when we ask for it?
- How can you seek the Lord and experience more of his grace this week?

Grades | A+++++

Title: A CHRISTMAS STORY (PG)
MGM, 1983

Scripture: Psalm 146:5-10
Alternate Take: Expectations (1 Kings 19:13-18)

START TIME:	34 minutes, 30 seconds
START CUE:	Ralph turns in his paper.
END TIME:	36 minutes, 15 seconds
END CUE:	Kids carry Ralph on their shoulders around the room.
DURATION:	1 minute, 45 seconds

Overview: Ralph daydreams that his teacher loves his paper and gives him an "A+++++."

Illustration: Grades take up a lot of time and energy (and generate a lot of prayer) in a teenager's life. Use this funny scene to help participants see that while God doesn't guarantee straight A's, he can bring peace to a stressed-out soul.

Questions

- **How does academic pressure affect you?**
  Read aloud Psalm 146:5-10.
- **God doesn't promise straight A's, but how can he help you with your grades?**
- **What prevents you from turning your stress about grades over to God?**
- **How can you start including God in your issues with grades?**

Grief | I CAN'T GO ON

Title: SAVE THE LAST DANCE (PG-13)
Paramount Pictures, 2001

Scripture: Psalm 116:1-8
Alternate Takes: Goals (Romans 8:24-28),
Selfishness (2 Corinthians 5:14-15)

START TIME:	58 minutes, 00 seconds
START CUE:	Sara and Derek exit the building.
END TIME:	1 hour, 1 minute, 00 seconds
END CUE:	Sara and Derek embrace.
DURATION:	3 minutes

Overview: Sara refuses to make ballet a part of her life because of her grief over her mother's death and the blame she places on herself for it. Derek insists it's not her fault and tells her she's got to try to make it into Juilliard if she really wants it.

Illustration: People deal with their grief in dozens of different ways—through blame, anger, sorrow, denial…This discussion can help participants see that God knows their grief and wants to comfort them during the dark times so they can emerge on the other side of sadness as new creatures.

Questions

- **When have you experienced grief in your life?**
- **What are some different ways people deal with their grief?**
  Read aloud Psalm 116:1-8.
- **What would keep a person, while experiencing grief, from crying out to God?**
- **How can God help you deal with intense feelings of sorrow?**
- **How can you help someone else deal with grief?**

Guilt | NO BIGGIE, IT'S JUST YOUR FAULT

Title: SISTER ACT (PG)
Touchstone Pictures, 1992

Scripture: Psalm 51:1-4

Alternate Takes: Prayer (James 4:2-3),
Helping Others (Proverbs 14:31)

START TIME:	1 hour, 21 minutes, 30 seconds
START CUE:	The nuns talk to a pilot.
END TIME:	1 hour, 22 minutes, 30 seconds
END CUE:	The nuns sit in the helicopter as it flies through the air.
DURATION:	1 minute

Overview: The nuns can't afford to rent a helicopter, so they shadow the pilot while praying for God's mercy on his soul even though he refused to help them in their time of need.

Illustration: Guilt takes many forms. Sometimes we carry it around with us and other times we use it to bend others to our will. Use this scene to discuss the many forms of guilt and how God frees us from its oppressive grip.

Questions

- **When was the last time you felt guilty and what happened?**
- **How did you overcome your guilty feelings?**
  Read aloud Psalm 51:1-4.
- **What are some causes for and types of guilt?**
- **Can a person gain freedom from guilt on his or her own? Why or why not?**
- **Why doesn't God want you to feel guilty, and how can you live a guilt-free life?**

Helping Others | ARE YOU OK?

Title: WHAT LIES BENEATH (PG-13)
DreamWorks SKG, 2000

Scripture: 1 John 3:16-18

Alternate Takes: Selflessness (Romans 12:10-16),
Community (Proverbs 27:10)

START TIME:	12 minutes, 15 seconds
START CUE:	Claire cries softly.
END TIME:	14 minutes, 30 seconds
END CUE:	Mrs. Fuer disappears.
DURATION:	2 minutes, 15 seconds

Overview: Claire hears someone crying on the other side of the fence, and she asks if she can help. Frantic and upset, Mrs. Fuer comments on the fence separating them and then suddenly leaves.

Illustration: There are people in need around us every day. Sometimes we turn a blind eye to them, or sometimes there's a barrier separating us. Yet God calls us to overcome these obstacles, take note of the needs around us, and help others in any way possible.

Questions

- **What prevents people from helping others in need?**
  Read aloud 1 John 3:16-18.
- **Are Christians typically known by their words or their actions? Explain.**
- **What are some practical ways we could perform deeds of love for hurting people?**
- **Who are some needy people you've ignored and how can you help them in the future?**

Title: WHILE YOU WERE SLEEPING (PG)
Hollywood Pictures, 1995

Scripture: Isaiah 56:1-5

Alternate Take: Helping Others (Colossians 3:12-15)

START TIME:	1 hour, 18 minutes, 45 seconds
START CUE:	Lucy enters the room.
END TIME:	1 hour, 20 minutes, 45 seconds
END CUE:	Peter says, "It's probably you."
DURATION:	2 minutes

Overview: Lucy says adults don't get to do heroic things. Peter confesses that he's never done anything heroic like Lucy. After all, she jumped in front of a train! Peter chased a purse snatcher once, but then faked a hamstring pull. Lucy says he's heroic because he gives up his seat on the train every day.

Illustration: What exactly makes someone a hero? Is it only people who rush into burning buildings, or could it be someone who simply gives up his or her seat to an elderly woman? Define what it means to be a hero, and challenge those in your ministry to live heroic lives for Christ.

Questions
- **Who are some people you consider to be heroic? What makes them heroes?** Read aloud Isaiah 56:1-5.
- **How can a person be heroic for God?**
- **Where do you see opportunities to fight for justice and righteousness around you?**
- **What are some simple ways you can become more heroic?**

Hidden Sin | **I'VE GOT NOTHING TO HIDE**

Title: MEET THE PARENTS (PG-13)
Universal Pictures, 2000

Scripture: Ecclesiastes 12:13-14

Alternate Takes: Integrity (James 5:12), Lying (Psalm 34:11-13)

START TIME:	38 minutes, 30 seconds
START CUE:	Jack says, "I heard a noise."
END TIME:	40 minutes, 45 seconds
END CUE:	Jack says, "Yes or no."
DURATION:	2 minutes, 15 seconds

Overview: Jack catches Greg snooping around his office, admiring his polygraph machine. Jack suggests that Greg try it on, and Greg reluctantly agrees, believing he has nothing to hide. Jack straps him in and starts grilling him.

Illustration: All people have cobwebs in the closet that they don't want the world to see. These "hidden sins" will eventually come to light, so it's usually better to shine the light of confession on them before they grow ultra-moldy, shoved in the corner of your soul.

Questions

- **What is something you did as a child that you wanted to hide? What happened?**
- **Why do people naturally try to hide things instead of confessing them?** Read aloud Ecclesiastes 12:13-14.
- **How does this promise make you feel?**
- **Why do we try to hide things from an all-knowing God?**
- **How would confessing your sins immediately to God or to others affect your life?**

The Holy Spirit | THAT'S A FIRE!

Title: CAST AWAY (PG-13)
20th Century Fox, 2000

Scripture: Acts 2:1-4

Alternate Take: Sharing Faith (Matthew 5:14-16)

START TIME:	1 hour, 11 minutes, 15 seconds
START CUE:	Chuck positions his two sticks.
END TIME:	1 hour, 12 minutes, 30 seconds
END CUE:	Chuck puts a palm frond on the fire.
DURATION:	1 minute, 15 seconds

Overview: Chuck works intently, rubbing two sticks in order to create a spark and fire. The wood eventually does light, and Chuck joyously creates a huge roaring fire.

Illustration: This is a great clip to use in sparking (groan) discussion on the Holy Spirit. While the Spirit doesn't get as much "coverage" in the Bible as the Father and the Son, the Spirit plays the largest role in our everyday life, serving as our counselor, strength, and seal.

Questions

- **What are some things you associate with fire?** Read aloud Acts 2:1-4.

- Why do you think the Holy Spirit appeared like fire this time and not like a dove or in some other form?
- How is the Holy Spirit made evident in someone's life?
- What are some ways you can feed the Spirit's fire in your life, moving from a little spark to a roaring bonfire?

Homeless People | SPARE A NICKEL?

Title: PAY IT FORWARD (PG-13)
Warner Bros., 2000

Scripture: Deuteronomy 15:7-8

Alternate Take: Helping Others (Psalm 41:1)

START TIME:	14 minutes, 15 seconds
START CUE:	Trevor stops his bike.
END TIME:	14 minutes, 45 seconds
END CUE:	A homeless man makes eye contact with Trevor.
DURATION:	30 seconds

Overview: Trevor rides his bike up to a shantytown of homeless people. He surveys their squalid conditions, trying to figure out a way to help them.

Illustration: Jesus told us that the poor would always be with us, but that doesn't mean we should ignore their needs. Discuss practical ways for young people to help the homeless around them, both individually and corporately.

Questions
- What are some reasons people end up homeless?
  Read aloud Deuteronomy 15:7-8.
- Does this passage mean you have to give money to anyone who asks you? Why or why not?
- What is our church doing to help the poor and needy? What are you doing?
- What are some practical and effective ways of helping homeless people?

Hope | LOOK CLOSELY, IT'S THERE

Title: ORANGE COUNTY (PG-13)
Paramount Pictures, 2002

Scripture: Psalm 131

Alternate Take: Family (Psalm 68:4-6)

START TIME:	1 hour, 3 minutes, 45 seconds
START CUE:	Skinner and Shaun sit in Skinner's office.
END TIME:	1 hour, 5 minutes, 45 seconds
END CUE:	Shaun nods his head.
DURATION:	2 minutes

Overview: Skinner praises Shaun's book. The characters appeared doomed on the surface but had deep connections and relationships underneath. Skinner felt the theme of the book was that there's hope in the middle of a screwed-up world.

Illustration: That's the Bible's theme: God offers hope in the midst of a screwed-up world. With the TV and Internet news spreading gloom 24/7/365, use this clip to expose the hope God offers those who trust in him.

Questions

- Do you think there's hope in this screwed-up world? Why or why not?
- How are hopeful people different from the hopeless?
- Why do so many people live without hope?
  Read aloud Psalm 131.
- How can a person place hope in an invisible, sometimes silent God?
- How can you help provide hope for hopeless people?

Human Life | WHAT ARE YOU WORTH?

Title: A CIVIL ACTION (PG-13)
Touchstone Pictures, 1998

Scripture: Psalm 8

Alternate Takes: Judging (John 8:15), Favoritism (James 2:1-4)

START TIME:	30 seconds
START CUE:	Jan pushes a man in a wheelchair.
END TIME:	1 minute, 15 seconds
END CUE:	The text "Based on a True Story" appears.
DURATION:	45 seconds

Overview: Jan explains the worth of a person in a court of law—in personal injury lawsuits, different factors determine the worth of a person, such as age, marital status, and occupation.

Illustration: The world constantly places different values on people's lives. Rich are worth more than poor, executives more than laborers, and celebrities more than common folks. Use this discussion to show that each and every human being holds significance and equal worth in God's eyes—enough worth that he sent Jesus to die for each one of them.

Questions

- **Do you think some people are worth more than others? Explain.**
- **What determines a person's worth in society?**
  Read aloud Psalm 8.
- **Why does God place so much value on each human life?**
- **How can the church show people—all people—that they have value in God's eyes?**
- **What must happen for you to start seeing people the way God sees them?**

Humility | WHO'S YOUR DADDY?

Title: REMEMBER THE TITANS (PG-13)
Walt Disney Productions, 2000

Scripture: 1 Peter 5:5-7
Alternate Takes: God's Sovereignty (Psalm 135:1-6), Spiritual Family (Matthew 12:46-50)

START TIME:	14 minutes, 45 seconds
START CUE:	Gerry approaches Coach Boone.
END TIME:	16 minutes, 45 seconds
END CUE:	Ray straightens his tie.
DURATION:	2 minutes

Overview: Gerry tells Coach Boone who should make the team and what positions they should play. Boone reminds Gerry that he is about to leave his mom to join his family on the football team's bus…and to join Coach Boone, his "daddy."

Illustration: It's better to humble yourself instead of having to experience humiliation at the hands of another. God's Word encourages us to show complete humility before God's throne. Yet many people today see humility as a weakness. Protect your young people from "foot-in-mouth" disease by discussing this overlooked virtue.

Questions

- **What makes a person humble?**
- **How does the world generally view humility?**
  Read aloud 1 Peter 5:5-7.
- **How does God view humility?**
- **How can you learn to become more humble this week?**

Idols | I WANT TO MARRY IT

Title: CAST AWAY (PG-13)
20th Century Fox, 2000

Scripture: 1 John 5:19-21

Alternate Take: Grief (John 11:30-35)

START TIME:	1 hour, 41 minutes, 00 seconds
START CUE:	Wilson falls loose.
END TIME:	1 hour, 44 minutes, 00 seconds
END CUE:	Chuck repeats, "I'm sorry, Wilson," over and over again.
DURATION:	3 minutes

Overview: Wilson falls into the ocean and floats away from the raft. Chuck wakes up and swims frantically after Wilson, but the rope connecting him to his raft isn't long enough. He ends up returning to his raft, weeping over his lost volleyball.

Illustration: We may not want to admit how attached we are to some of our possessions. Yet often the material losses we might weep over can become potential idols in our lives. Use this clip to examine modern idolatry, and discuss safeguards people can take to firmly place God alone on the throne of their hearts.

Questions

- **What possessions or hobbies would you cry about if you had to give them up?** Read aloud 1 John 5:19-21.
- **What types of things or activities can people set up as idols in their lives?**
- **What determines if something is an idol in a person's life?**
- **What has the potential to become an idol in your life, and how can you guard against that happening?**

Illness | THINGS DON'T LOOK GOOD

Title: AS GOOD AS IT GETS (PG-13)
TriStar Pictures, 1997

Scripture: James 5:14-15

Alternate Take: Compassion (Job 2:11-13)

START TIME:	22 minutes, 00 seconds
START CUE:	Melvin smiles.
END TIME:	23 minutes, 15 seconds
END CUE:	Carol leaves with the plates.
DURATION:	1 minute, 15 seconds

Overview: Melvin asks Carol what's wrong with her son. Carol hesitantly reveals that her son has asthma and a low immune system.

Illustration: Serious medical problems touch every life periodically, and God's children should be on the front lines comforting, caring, and praying for the sick. Explore ways to deal with illness and to help others cope with it.

Questions
- **How do you typically deal with sickness or the illness of someone else?**
- **Why does God let people get sick?**
  Read aloud James 5:14-15.
- **Why might someone not get well even if you pray for them?**
- **How can you comfort someone who is sick or dealing with illness in his or her family?**

Imitating Christ | SHOULD I GROW OUT MY HAIR?

Title: RUSH HOUR 2 (PG-13)
New Line Cinema, 2001

Scripture: Romans 13:12-14

Alternate Take: Blasphemy (Leviticus 24:10-12)

START TIME:	5 minutes, 00 seconds
START CUE:	Carter says, "How ya doin'?"
END TIME:	7 minutes, 30 seconds
END CUE:	Carter sings, "I'll be right back."
DURATION:	2 minutes, 30 seconds

Overview: Carter can't believe the "sacrilegious" karaoke rendition of Michael Jackson that someone is performing on stage. He takes over the mic and executes a perfect song and dance imitation of the gloved one.

Illustration: Thankfully, Jesus didn't moonwalk or keep a monkey named Bubbles! Use this discussion to show teenagers that God's children should attempt to imitate their king as closely as possible, learning to act like their Savior and providing a living representation for the world.

Questions

- **What is your best imitation of someone else? Demonstrate it.**
  Read aloud Romans 13:12-14.
- **How can people clothe themselves with Christ?**
- **Why should we try to imitate Christ if he was perfect and we aren't?**
- **What is one way you can try to imitate Christ this week?**

The Inner City | IN THE GHETTO

Title: HARDBALL (PG-13)
Paramount Pictures, 2001

Scripture: Proverbs 31:8-9
Alternate Takes: Violence (Job 24:2-16), Poverty (Proverbs 10:15)

START TIME:	42 minutes, 30 seconds
START CUE:	The car drives up to the projects.
END TIME:	43 minutes, 45 seconds
END CUE:	Andre closes the door.
DURATION:	1 minute, 15 seconds

Overview: Andre asks if Conor wants to see his home. Conor follows him into the projects and asks why people sit on the floors. Andre explains that it keeps them below the window and stray bullets.

Illustration: Those who live in the inner city face some dire problems and seemingly insurmountable odds that others from suburban and rural areas often don't understand. God is present and active amongst his people, even in the midst of the poverty and violence that plagues the inner city. Use this scene to help teenagers think about some of the issues related to inner-city life and discover ways they can make a difference through prayer and other means.

Questions

- **What are some of the problems plaguing the inner city?**
- **What reasons do people have for not dealing with inner-city problems?**
  Read aloud Proverbs 31:8-9.
- **How can the church minister to inner-city residents?**
- **What are some practical ways we can help as a ministry? as individuals?**

Title: A WALK TO REMEMBER (PG)
Warner Bros., 2002

Scripture: John 3:1-2

Alternate Takes: Friends (2 Timothy 4:16-17),
Cliques (1 Corinthians 12:22-27)

START TIME:	29 minutes, 30 seconds
START CUE:	Kids exit the front door of the school.
END TIME:	31 minutes, 30 seconds
END CUE:	Jamie closes the door on Landon.
DURATION:	2 minutes

Warning! *A swear word is said soon after the End Cue for this clip, so make sure to stop the movie at the right time.*

Overview: Landon brushes Jamie off in front of his friends. Later he goes to her house, pretending as if nothing happened. Jamie rejects him, letting him know that she doesn't want to be "secret friends."

Illustration: Too many people try to live double lives, projecting different images of themselves depending on the situation. This dearth of integrity is seen too often within our country's schools, boardrooms, pulpits, and political meetings. Use this scene to help students see that in order to affect change, God's people must model integrity for a fallen world.

Questions

- Who do you relate to in this scene and why?
- Why didn't Landon acknowledge Jamie at school?
  Read aloud John 3:1-2.
- Why did Nicodemus go to Jesus at night? Does this reveal anything about his integrity? Explain.
- Why is integrity so important?
- How can you strengthen your integrity?

Jealousy | MARSHA, MARSHA, MARSHA!

Title: A LEAGUE OF THEIR OWN (PG)
Columbia Pictures, 1992

Scripture: Proverbs 6:34-35

Alternate Takes: Favoritism (Genesis 25:21-28),
Jacob and Esau (Genesis 25:29-34)

START TIME:	9 minutes, 45 seconds
START CUE:	A tractor drives across the field.
END TIME:	11 minutes, 15 seconds
END CUE:	The girls run to the barn.
DURATION:	1 minute, 30 seconds

Overview: Kit feels like everyone loves her older sister, Dottie, and no one appreciates her.

Illustration: Sometimes rivalries are never stronger than between family members. While competition isn't necessarily bad, use this clip to encourage teenagers to be cautious about letting competition deteriorate into jealousy.

Questions
- **What makes you jealous?**
- **What do you do with your jealous feelings?**
  Read aloud Proverbs 6:34-35.
- **What makes jealousy such a strong emotion?**
- **How can you get rid of jealousy?**

Jesus' Death | ONE IN THE GUT

Title: PAY IT FORWARD (PG-13)
Warner Bros., 2000

Scripture: John 19:28-37

Alternate Take: Sacrifice (John 15:13)

START TIME:	1 hour, 51 minutes, 45 seconds
START CUE:	Trevor gets his bike.
END TIME:	1 hour, 53 minutes, 15 seconds
END CUE:	Trevor lies dead on the ground.
DURATION:	1 minute, 30 seconds

Overview: Bullies attack Adam. He cries out for help, and Trevor comes to his aid. Adam gets away but not before one of the bullies stabs Trevor with a switchblade.

Illustration: This clip serves as a symbol of what Jesus Christ did for us. We were beat up by Satan, shackled by sin, and Jesus came in and took the fatal blow on our behalf. Help your young people view Jesus' heroic sacrifice through a modern context with this powerful scene.

Questions

- **Would you help a stranger in need, even if it was dangerous? Why or why not?**

  Read aloud John 19:28-37.

- **How does the movie clip mirror what Christ did for us?**
- **Why would Jesus die for people he knew would reject him?**
- **What is your response to Jesus' sacrifice for you on the cross and how does it affect your life?**

Judging | JUST LOOK AT THE COVER

Title: THE SPITFIRE GRILL (PG-13)
Columbia Pictures, 1996

Scripture: John 7:24

Alternate Takes: Discernment (Isaiah 11:2-4), Confession (Leviticus 5:5-6)

START TIME:	1 hour, 42 minutes, 45 seconds
START CUE:	A man plays the organ.
END TIME:	1 hour, 45 minutes, 30 seconds
END CUE:	Nahum leaves the podium.
DURATION:	2 minutes, 45 seconds

Overview: Nahum stands up to speak at Percy's funeral. He confesses that he never knew Percy, even though he thought he did. He judged her and took money before she could steal it. He thought he knew her, but he was wrong.

Illustration: Judging others by external characteristics—such as appearance and social status—comes almost as easily as blinking and breathing. As Christians we don't have the luxury of judging others, though, since that's up to God alone. Use this clip to encourage participants to look below the surface of another's skin before making any character judgments.

Questions

- Have you ever misjudged someone? What happened?
- What are the negative effects of judging a person without knowing him or her?

Read aloud John 7:24.

- What does "right judgment" mean?
- How can you learn not to judge someone by his or her outward appearance?

King Nebuchadnezzar | I WAS A CONTENDER

Title: HOOP DREAMS (PG-13)
Fine Line Features, 1994

Scripture: Daniel 4:28-37

Alternate Take: Pride (Proverbs 16:5)

START TIME:	33 minutes, 00 seconds
START CUE:	Curtis says, "I know a whole lot about basketball."
END TIME:	34 minutes, 45 seconds
END CUE:	Curtis tickets some cars.
DURATION:	1 minute, 45 seconds

Overview: Curtis once had an amazing basketball career but believed that good players could do whatever they want. Coaches stopped playing him despite his phenomenal talent. Eventually, Curtis quit basketball and became a security guard.

Illustration: Though this change is not as drastic as Nebuchadnezzar's metamorphosis from king-status to insanity, this tragic true story reveals the ugly side of pride and how it can bring a high-flying individual crashing to the ground.

Questions

- How have you seen prideful people crash and burn?

Read aloud Daniel 4:28-37.

- How does a person become prideful like King Nebuchadnezzar?
- Why doesn't God do something like this to all prideful people?
- How can you guard yourself from Nebuchadnezzar-like pride?

Title: LEFT BEHIND: THE MOVIE (PG)
Cloud Ten, 2001

Scripture: Matthew 24:34-41
Alternate Take: Assurance (1 Thessalonians 5:1-8)

START TIME:	26 minutes, 30 seconds
START CUE:	An old woman wakes up.
END TIME:	29 minutes, 30 seconds
END CUE:	The crazy man gets tackled.
DURATION:	3 minutes

Overview: An old woman asks Buck to look in the bathroom for her missing husband, pointing to his pile of clothes beside her. Passengers freak out when they notice their children and loved ones missing from their seats, with only piles of clothes left behind.

Illustration: There's a lot of pop culture and religious fervor surrounding the idea of the Last Days. Use this clip to start a discussion on what the Bible has to say about this topic and to launch into an analysis of the various Christian perspectives.

Questions

- **Why are people so interested in the Last Days?**
  Read aloud Matthew 24:34-41
- **What kinds of things do people say will happen in the Last Days? What does the Bible say?**
- **When you think about the Last Days, how does it make you feel? Why?**
- **How should what you believe about the Last Days affect your life and relationship with God?**

Legalism | **RULE #327**

Title: THE HUDSUCKER PROXY (PG)
Warner Bros., 1994

Scripture: Romans 9:30-10:4
Alternate Take: Mentoring (Ephesians 4:11-16)

START TIME:	13 minutes, 00 seconds
START CUE:	The doors fly open.
END TIME:	14 minutes, 15 seconds
END CUE:	"And they dock ya!"
DURATION:	1 minute, 15 seconds

Overview: Norville gets a crash course on the million and one rules and regulations he must follow in his job in order not to have the company dock his pay.

Illustration: Unfortunately, a lot of people approach God's laws this way. ("God's got a list of rules ten miles long, and anyone who misses a jot or tittle gets punished immediately!") Encourage participants to find freedom from the shackles of legalism by connecting to God's grace and seeking guidance from his Holy Spirit.

Questions

- **What are some rules Christians live by that aren't in the Bible?**
- **Why do people want to live by rules?**
  Read aloud Romans 9:30–10:4.
- **Why doesn't God consider a person righteous for pursuing the Law?**
- **Can a person receive God's grace without obeying God's laws? Explain.**
- **What's the difference between obedience and legalism?**

Legalism | FOLLOW THE RULES!

Title: THE MAJESTIC (PG)
Warner Bros., 2001

Scripture: Romans 3:19-24
Alternate Take: Petition (Philippians 4:6-7)

START TIME:	1 hour, 19 minutes, 00 seconds
START CUE:	The city council meeting scene begins.
END TIME:	1 hour, 20 minutes, 00 seconds
END CUE:	The mayor says, "Go ahead, son."
DURATION:	1 minute

Overview: The Trimbles ask the city council for help. A townsperson protests because their motion is out of order. The mayor quickly goes through the motions of voting and approving the agenda change in order to follow the letter of the law.

Illustration: The Law should convict people and point them to God, not oppress them. Challenge your youth to follow the spirit of the Law instead of worrying about imposing the Law on themselves and others. Use this discussion to help teenagers understand that legalism stifles the grace we find in the gospel.

Questions

- **Do you think God is more like the townsperson or the mayor when it comes to rules? Why?**

- **What are some Christian rules you think are too legalistic? Why?**
  Read aloud Romans 3:19-24.
- **Does this mean we don't have to follow God's laws? Why or why not?**
- **What might motivate a person to live legalistically?**
- **How can you obey God without becoming legalistic?**

Lies | IT KEEPS GROWING...

Title: WHERE THE HEART IS (PG-13)
20th Century Fox, 2000

Scripture: Psalm 34:12-13

Alternate Takes: Mistakes (Psalm 51:1-4),
Forgiveness (Mark 11:25)

START TIME:	1 hour, 46 minutes, 30 seconds
START CUE:	Willy Jack lies in a hospital bed.
END TIME:	1 hour, 49 minutes, 30 seconds
END CUE:	Novalee says she understands.
DURATION:	3 minutes

Overview: Novalee visits Willy Jack in the hospital. Willy apologizes for lying to her years ago about their baby. He says that he *could* feel the baby's heartbeat, and that lie changed his entire life for the worse. He wishes he could do something to change what he had said and done.

Illustration: Popular wisdom treats "small" lies and "tiny" untruths as if they're no big deal as long as they don't hurt anybody. In the long run, though, those little fibs have some big consequences! Use this clip to help participants see that someone can always seek and hopefully find forgiveness in the cold spotlight of truth, but they can't erase the consequences or the damage their lies have done.

Questions
- **Have you ever been caught in or admitted a lie? What happened?**
  Read aloud Psalm 34:12-13.
- **How can telling lies hurt the quality of your life? How can lying hurt others?**
- **What motivates people to tell lies, and what are some of the consequences?**
- **What area of your life do you need to become more honest about?**

Life | CARPE DIEM

Title: DEAD POETS SOCIETY (PG)
Touchstone Pictures, 1989

Scripture: Ecclesiastes 3:18-22
Alternate Take: Death (Psalm 39:4-5)

START TIME:	13 minutes, 45 seconds
START CUE:	The students open their books.
END TIME:	16 minutes, 30 seconds
END CUE:	Professor Keating whispers, "Make your lives extraordinary."
DURATION:	2 minutes, 45 seconds

Overview: Professor Keating tells his students to *carpe diem*—seize the day. He reminds them that every person's days are numbered and everyone eventually dies. He has his class look at the pictures of past students who now lie dead, then challenges his current students to make the most of their lives.

Illustration: Life is a precious gift that far too many squander on empty pursuits or mindless vegetation (movies not included). We should use every moment of life pursuing God and his kingdom! Challenge those in your ministry to "seize the day" and joyfully seek the things of God.

Questions
- Do you feel as if you *"carpe diem"*? Why or why not?
- What kinds of things prevent people from "seizing the day"?
  Read aloud Ecclesiastes 3:18-22.
- What makes people think they're going to live forever?
- What are the worthy pursuits in your life? the unworthy pursuits?
- How should you change your life so you are "seizing the day" for God?

Listening | WHAT?

Title: WHAT WOMEN WANT (PG-13)
Paramount Pictures, 2000

Scripture: Matthew 17:5-6
Alternate Take: Parents (Colossians 3:21)

START TIME:	26 minutes, 30 seconds
START CUE:	Alex and Cameron catch Nick.
END TIME:	28 minutes, 00 seconds
END CUE:	Nick returns to the bathroom.
DURATION:	1 minute, 30 seconds

Overview: Nick meets Cameron. Alex chastises Nick for never listening to her. He defends himself but loses the battle when he can't remember Cameron's name.

Illustration: Many times we're so concerned about ourselves that we completely miss what friends, family, and even God are saying to us. Use this discussion to teach teenagers some practical listening skills.

Questions
- **Why is listening so hard?**
  Read aloud Matthew 17:5-6.
- **Why do you think God had to tell the disciples to listen to Jesus?**
- **Why don't people today listen to what Jesus says?**
- **How do you know when God is speaking to you?**
- **What are some practical ways to improve your spiritual hearing?**

The Lord's Name | NO VANITY, PLEASE

Title: HOOP DREAMS (PG-13)
Fine Line Features, 1994

Scripture: Exodus 20:7

Alternate Take: Prayer (Matthew 6:5-6)

START TIME:	1 hour, 42 minutes, 45 seconds
START CUE:	The locker room hall.
END TIME:	1 hour, 43 minutes, 30 seconds
END CUE:	The team exits the locker room.
DURATION:	45 seconds

Overview: The coach reams out his team before leading them through a hurried, lackluster prayer.

Illustration: Taking the Lord's name in vain isn't reserved only for choice swear words. Using it to try to manipulate God or others is the ultimate vanity. Show your youth how people misuse God's name and the importance of always showing God reverence.

Questions
- **Does God listen to prayers like this? Why or why not?**
  Read aloud Exodus 20:7.
- **What are some ways you can misuse the name of the Lord?**
- **Why do people take God's name so lightly in speech and attitude?**
- **How have you been misusing God's name, and how can you give him the reverence he deserves?**

Love | THE GREATEST THING

Title: MOULIN ROUGE! (PG-13)
20th Century Fox, 2001

Scripture: 1 Corinthians 13

Alternate Take: Depression (Psalm 42)

START TIME:	1 minute, 00 seconds
START CUE:	Text reads "Paris, 1900."
END TIME:	3 minutes, 15 seconds
END CUE:	Christian types "The Moulin Rouge."
DURATION:	2 minutes, 15 seconds

Overview: Toulouse Lautrec sings of a man who lives in squalid circumstances and believes, "The greatest thing you'll ever learn is to love and be loved in return."

Illustration: A vast amount of human art and pursuit centers on love. While people can sing about, dream of, and even pay for love, it remains a confusing word. Set the record straight with Paul's description of perfect love.

Questions

- **How do you define love?**
- **If love is such an important thing, why do people have so many different ideas about what it is?**

  Read aloud 1 Corinthians 13.
- **What are the core values of God's definition of love?**
- **How is this definition different from the world's definition?**
- **How does God's definition alter your view of love?**

Media Messages | OUR GREATEST TEACHER

Title: ZOOLANDER (PG-13)
Paramount Pictures, 2001

Scripture: Proverbs 2:6-12

Alternate Takes: Helping Others (Matthew 25:32-40), Beauty (1 Peter 3:3-4)

START TIME:	13 minutes, 15 seconds
START CUE:	Zoolander's apartment building.
END TIME:	14 minutes, 30 seconds
END CUE:	Zoolander says, "I guess so."
DURATION:	1 minute, 15 seconds

Overview: Meekus and Brint start arguing when Zoolander asks, "Isn't there more to life than being good looking?" He thinks they should help people. They reply that they *do* help people by making them feel good and showing them how to dress and style their hair.

Illustration: The media, especially advertising, convinces viewers to strive for fantasy lives by depicting models who subliminally proclaim that pure joy comes from owning particular products, wearing particular clothes, or possessing a particular body. Help your young people understand that God is the only source of genuine contentment, joy, and peace—not life in TV La-La Land.

Questions

- **What underlying messages do models in TV commercials and magazines send?**
- **What false media messages have fooled you in the past?**
  Read aloud Proverbs 2:6-12.
- **How does God's wisdom protect us from false media messages?**
- **What can we do to increase our knowledge of God?**

Miracles | I DIDN'T SEE NOTHIN'

Title: O BROTHER, WHERE ART THOU? (PG-13)
Touchstone Pictures, 2000

Scripture: John 9:1-38

Alternate Takes: Spiritual Blindness (Matthew 13:13-17), Pharaoh (Exodus 7:8-23)

START TIME:	1 hour, 39 minutes, 00 seconds
START CUE:	Everett surfaces.
END TIME:	1 hour, 40 minutes, 45 seconds
END CUE:	Everett repeats, "Not a moment too soon."
DURATION:	1 minute, 45 seconds

Overview: The guys surface from the depths of the sudden flood. Delmar proclaims the event a miracle, but Everett dismisses what happened through his own "logical" explanation. He claims that the age of reason will do away with superstitions, then trails off when a cow floats by on the roof of a house.

Illustration: God still performs miracles, but does anyone notice? Use this clip to discuss miracles, how God used them in the Bible, whether he uses them now, and how we can become sensitive to moments of divine intervention in modern life.

Questions

- Have you ever witnessed a miracle? If so, what happened?
- What's the difference between a miracle and a coincidence?
  Read aloud John 9:1-38.
- Does God still perform miracles like this today? Why or why not?
- How can you learn to notice the miracles that happen around you?

Mission | WHAT'S THE GOAL?

Title: PEARL HARBOR (PG-13)
Touchstone Pictures, 2001

Scripture: Luke 24:45-49

Alternate Takes: Victory (Deuteronomy 20:1-4), Dedication (Exodus 32:29)

START TIME:	Tape/Disc 2, 16 minutes, 45 seconds
START CUE:	Rafe and Danny stand at the edge of the carrier.
END TIME:	Tape/Disc 2, 18 minutes, 00 seconds
END CUE:	Doolittle walks away.
DURATION:	1 minute, 15 seconds

Overview: Rafe and Danny ask Doolittle what exactly they're dying for. The colonel says their bombing raid will only be a pinprick but that it will pierce through the hearts of the Japanese. Victory belongs to those who believe the most and the longest.

Illustration: Use this scene to give some direction and vision to your "troops," laying out what the mission is for God's children so they understand the cause and have something solid to give their lives for.

Questions

- What is our mission as followers of Jesus Christ?
  Read aloud Luke 24:45-49.
- Do you think our church is doing a good job of following Jesus' mission? Explain.
- What obstacles stand in the way of carrying out our mission?
- What are some methods for better carrying out our mission as individuals? as a group?

Missionaries | I'M EATING *WHAT*?!?!

Title: INDIANA JONES AND THE TEMPLE OF DOOM (PG)
Paramount Pictures, 1984

Scripture: 1 Corinthians 9:19-23

Alternate Take: Hospitality (Hebrews 13:2)

START TIME:	21 minutes, 30 seconds
START CUE:	The villagers bring food.
END TIME:	22 minutes, 30 seconds
END CUE:	Indy asks for a guide.
DURATION:	1 minute

Overview: Willie declines to eat the villagers' food. Indy tells her it's rude to refuse their generosity because the people themselves are starving. She grudgingly eats the food.

Illustration: Christ's missionaries (that's you and me too) must graciously accept the kindness of the people they seek to serve, no matter how repulsive or bizarre the situation. We must prepare our hearts (and stomachs) for becoming all things to all people on the mission field.

Questions

- **What is the most repulsive thing you've ever had to eat?**
- **What are some bizarre things missionaries might be asked to do or eat in order to respect local customs?**
  Read aloud 1 Corinthians 9:19-23.
- **Why must a missionary be willing to do things outside of his or her comfort zone?**
- **How can you prepare yourself to be a light for all people in all situations, whether on the mission field or in everyday life?**

Moses | YOU MUST BE MISTAKEN

Title: THE PRINCE OF EGYPT (PG)
DreamWorks SKG, 1998

Scripture: Exodus 3:1-10

Alternate Takes: Confidence (Numbers 23:19),
God (Exodus 3:13-17)

START TIME:	44 minutes, 15 seconds
START CUE:	Moses says, "Here I am."
END TIME:	47 minutes, 15 seconds
END CUE:	God says, "I shall be with you, Moses."
DURATION:	3 minutes

Overview: Moses encounters the burning bush and meets God, the great I AM. God sends Moses to free Israel from slavery, but Moses says he can't do it. God forcefully declares that Moses can do it because God will be with him.

Illustration: This scene breathes new life into the burning bush that graces flannel graphs across the country. Use it to discuss the reluctant leader who learned to totally trust in God's promises.

Questions

- **Why did God choose Moses, out of all the people in the world, to deliver Israel?**

    Read aloud Exodus 3:1-10.

- **Why did God ask Moses to do something he could never accomplish on his own?**

- **Has God ever spoken to you? If yes, how did you know?**

- **What factors made it difficult for Moses to believe God?**

- **How can you build up your faith now so you're ready to step out boldly, as Moses did, when God speaks to you?**

Natural Disasters | WHY US?

Title: TWISTER (PG-13)
Warner Bros., 1996

Scripture: Romans 8:35-39
Alternate Takes: Tragedy (Joel 1:2-5),
Helping Others (Luke 16:19-21)

START TIME:	1 hour, 18 minutes, 15 seconds
START CUE:	A sign reads "Welcome to Wakita."
END TIME:	1 hour, 20 minutes, 30 seconds
END CUE:	Jo says, "We're here, we're coming down!"
DURATION:	2 minutes, 15 seconds

Overview: The team drives through a town leveled by a tornado. They observe the complete destruction of property and loss of life caused by the storm.

Illustration: There's never a comforting answer for why natural disasters happen. Many question God's existence when they're faced with such a tragedy. Use this scene to give those in your ministry a solid foundation for facing nature's wrath and for finding ways to share God's love in the midst of heartache.

Questions

- **What are some natural disasters you know of, and how have they affected people?**

Read aloud Romans 8:35-39.

- **Why do people feel separated from or condemned by God during natural disasters?**
- **Where is God in the midst of natural disasters?**
- **How can a person feel God's care, or share God's love with others in the midst of extreme devastation?**

Needs | I DON'T *NEED* IT

Title: FATHER OF THE BRIDE (PG)
Touchstone Pictures, 1991

Scripture: Luke 12:29-31

Alternate Take: Anger (Ecclesiastes 7:9)

START TIME:	57 minutes, 30 seconds
START CUE:	George stands in the hot dog bun aisle.
END TIME:	59 minutes, 15 seconds
END CUE:	George runs around the corner.
DURATION:	1 minute, 45 seconds

Overview: George refuses to buy another thing that he doesn't need. He removes four hot dog buns from the package of twelve, then runs out of the store.

Illustration: Sometimes it's hard to discern between our wants and needs. We often end up with extra stuff we don't need (and maybe didn't even want). Even though you might always get stuck with more hot dog buns than you need, you can still use this discussion to define what needs truly are.

Questions

- **What's the last thing you bought that you didn't need? Why did you buy it?**
- **How do you discern the difference between something you need and something you want?**

Read aloud Luke 12:29-31.

- **What are the basic needs of humanity?**
- **Is it OK to pursue things you don't need? Why or why not?**
- **How can you learn to be content in life even if you don't have everything you want?**

New Life | YOU LOOK DIFFERENT

Title: THE HUDSUCKER PROXY (PG)
Warner Bros., 1994

Scripture: Matthew 5:13-16
Alternate Take: Sharing Faith (1 Peter 2:9-12)

START TIME:	1 hour, 5 minutes, 30 seconds
START CUE:	A shopkeeper throws Hula-Hoops out into the alley.
END TIME:	1 hour, 7 minutes, 30 seconds
END CUE:	The shopkeeper slaps a "$3.99" sticker on the Hula-Hoops.
DURATION:	2 minutes

Overview: A Hula-Hoop rolls through the streets and lands in front of a little boy. He picks it up and starts "Hula-Hooping" like a freak! Kids stop and stare in awe and then rush to the store to buy their own.

Illustration: Christians should stand out in a crowd (and not just because they're wearing a Christian T-shirt). People should not only notice a difference, but should *want* to be like us. Discuss what it means to exhibit new life and practical ways to live in a manner that attracts others to Christ.

Questions

- Do people usually notice something different about your life? Why or why not?
- How should a Christian's life be different from other people's? Read aloud Matthew 5:13-16.
- What kinds of things attract people to Jesus Christ?
- What are some practical ways to shine your light for others?

Obstacles to Growth | YOU CAN'T LEAVE

Title: MOULIN ROUGE! (PG-13)
20th Century Fox, 2001

Scripture: 2 Corinthians 4:1-4
Alternate Takes: Death (James 4:13-14), Love (1 Corinthians 13)

START TIME:	1 hour, 27 minutes, 30 seconds
START CUE:	Satine rushes around packing.
END TIME:	1 hour, 29 minutes, 30 seconds
END CUE:	Fade to black.
DURATION:	2 minutes

Overview: Harold informs Satine that she must become the duke's lover or Christian will be killed. Satine refuses, asserting the fact that Christian truly loves her as a person rather than as an object. Then Harold drops the bomb about Satine's terminal illness, telling her there's no future for her outside the Moulin Rouge.

Illustration: Jesus promises unconditional love, but Satan traps people in his "Moulin Rouge" by intimidating, confusing, and convincing them that Jesus can't really love them. Discuss this clip to help others reject Satan's lies by clinging to the pure love of Jesus Christ.

Questions

- **How is Christian's love for Satine like Jesus' love for us?**
- **What obstacles can prevent people from growing spiritually?**
  Read aloud 2 Corinthians 4:1-4.
- **Why does God allow Satan to blind unbelievers?**
- **What are some of the lies Satan tells people so they will reject Jesus' love?**
- **How can you help introduce someone to new life in Jesus?**

Omnipotence | MY DAD CAN BEAT ALL DADS

Title: THE PRINCE OF EGYPT (PG)
DreamWorks SKG, 1998

Scripture: Psalm 93

Alternate Takes: Deliverance (Psalm 3), Miracles (Psalm 77:13-14)

START TIME:	1 hour, 22 minutes, 30 seconds
START CUE:	The Egyptian army races over the hill.
END TIME:	1 hour, 24 minutes, 45 seconds
END CUE:	Aaron crosses on dry land.
DURATION:	2 minutes, 15 seconds

Overview: God protects the Israelites from the Egyptian army with a wall of fire. Moses then parts the Red Sea with his staff.

Illustration: Sometimes we forget the awesome power of the living God! Sit in awe of this computer animation, and let that majesty propel a conversation about the incredible might of our God.

Questions

- **What images does the word *omnipotent* bring to your mind?**
  Read aloud Psalm 93.
- **What are some of the ways God demonstrates his omnipotence?**

- Why does an omnipotent God want a relationship with us?
- What effect does our omnipotent God have on your everyday life?

Origins | IT ALL STARTED WITH...

Title: PLANET OF THE APES (PG-13)
20th Century Fox, 2001

Scripture: Nehemiah 9:6

Alternate Take: Scripture (Psalm 119:89-92)

START TIME:	Tape/Disc 1, 59 minutes, 45 seconds
START CUE:	The group finds the freaky scarecrows.
END TIME:	Tape/Disc 1, 1 hour, 00 minutes, 45 seconds
END CUE:	Limbo says, "Doesn't he ever stop?"
DURATION:	1 minute

Overview: Krull explains that the creator breathed life into Simos, the first at the sacred city of Calima. Ari scoffs, saying that it's only a metaphor to explain creation and that there never was a Simos.

Illustration: The debate over the origins of life won't be settled until we're all in heaven (and we won't really care much about it then). Sidestep the sticking points and attack the heart of the matter—God as the divine force behind creation. Help your young people see the importance of God's hand in our origins.

Questions
- **Where do science and faith seem to disagree on the origins of life?**
  Read aloud Nehemiah 9:6.
- **What is the core truth about the origins of creation according to this verse?**
- **Why is a belief in God as the originator of creation so important to faith?**
- **How can you integrate your faith knowledgeably into future conversations about the origins of life?**

Parents | YOU *WILL* BE A DOCTOR!

Title: BRING IT ON (PG-13)
Universal Pictures, 2000

Scripture: Exodus 20:12

Alternate Takes: Priorities (Matthew 6:26-34),
Pressure (Psalm 72:12-14)

START TIME:	8 minutes, 30 seconds
START CUE:	Torr enters the kitchen and says, "I got captain."
END TIME:	9 minutes, 30 seconds
END CUE:	Torr agrees with her mother.
DURATION:	1 minute

Overview: Torr tells her mom and Justin that she made cheerleading captain. Then her mom gets on Torr's case about how she prioritizes cheerleading over her studies. Torr agrees to take chemistry to please her mother.

Illustration: Parents have always got an opinion…and a lot of times they're good ones. Whether they are or not doesn't matter as much as our attitude towards our parents. We must honor our parents, so help participants figure out exactly what that means and how that plays out in real life.

Questions

- **How would you describe your relationship with your parents?**
  Read aloud Exodus 20:12.
- **Why did God make honoring your parents one of the Ten Commandments?**
- **What exactly does honor mean?**
- **How can you honor your parents without always agreeing with them?**
- **How do you need to start honoring your parents more?**

Passover | BLOOD ON THE DOORPOST

Title: THE PRINCE OF EGYPT (PG)
DreamWorks SKG, 1998

Scripture: Exodus 12:1-14

Alternate Takes: Death (Psalm 89:47-48), Judgment (Ecclesiastes 12:13-14)

START TIME:	1 hour, 12 minutes, 15 seconds
START CUE:	The camera pans down on the city.
END TIME:	1 hour, 15 minutes, 00 seconds
END CUE:	The angel of death disappears.
DURATION:	2 minutes, 45 seconds

Overview: Moses explains the Passover and commands the Hebrews to spread blood around their doors for protection. They wait inside as the angel of death passes through Egypt.

Illustration: God instituted Passover as a sign of his deliverance and mercy. Use this scene to introduce this important Jewish holiday and to help teenagers see exactly what meaning it holds for God's children today.

Questions

- Why don't Christians typically celebrate Passover?
  Read aloud Exodus 12:1-14.
- What is the symbolism of the different elements of Passover?
- What significance does Passover hold for Christians?
- How does Passover exemplify God's love for you and the entire world?

The Past | NO ONE FORGETS

Title: MY DOG SKIP (PG)
Warner Bros., 2000

Scripture: Jeremiah 31:33-34
Alternate Take: Labels (Matthew 11:18-19)

START TIME:	1 hour, 16 minutes, 30 seconds
START CUE:	Jack talks to Dink.
END TIME:	1 hour, 18 minutes, 15 seconds
END CUE:	Dink leaves.
DURATION:	1 minute, 45 seconds

Overview: Jack tells Dink that people will eventually forget a person's past. Dink doesn't believe they'll ever forget that he's a coward. Jack explains that no matter what people say, Dink will always be a hero to Willie.

Illustration: Everyone makes mistakes, but some are harder to live down than others. Use this clip to reinforce the fact that God forgives our past when we ask him to. We should do the same for those around us.

Questions

- What makes past mistakes so hard to leave behind?
- Why do people like to remind others of their past mistakes?
  Read aloud Jeremiah 31:33-34.
- If God forgets the past, why can't we forget our own?
- What needs to happen for you to overcome your past mistakes?
- How can we support people who've made mistakes in their past?

Paul's Conversion | LEAVING THE COCOON

Title: DR. SUESS' HOW THE GRINCH
STOLE CHRISTMAS (PG)
Universal Pictures, 2000

Scripture: Acts 9:1-20

Alternate Take: New Life (1 John 5:1-5)

START TIME:	1 hour, 24 minutes, 00 seconds
START CUE:	The narrator says, "Then the Grinch thought of something…"
END TIME:	1 hour, 27 minutes, 00 seconds
END CUE:	The Grinch says, "Max, I love you!"
DURATION:	3 minutes

Overview: The Grinch realizes Christmas is about more than "stuff." He yells in
pain as his heart actually starts beating and he starts feeling for the first time.
His heart grows three times until he feels all "toasty inside."

Illustration: This is a humorous analogy to Paul's conversion. The Grinch, like
Paul, gets knocked off his feet unexpectedly with a new heart and must move
into a radical new way of life filled with God's grace.

Questions

- **How was the Grinch's experience like a spiritual conversion?**
  Read aloud Acts 9:1-20.
- **Can a person meet Jesus and not experience a radical difference in his or
  her life? Explain.**
- **Why did God choose Saul (later called Paul) to be a missionary to the
  Gentiles?**
- **Why does God meet people in different ways?**
- **How did God meet you, and how does he want to use you for his kingdom?**

Peer Pressure | JOIN US

Title: ORANGE COUNTY (PG-13)
Paramount Pictures, 2002

Scripture: 1 Corinthians 15:33-34

Alternate Take: Death (James 4:13-14)

START TIME:	1 minute, 15 seconds
START CUE:	Shaun reads a book in the library.
END TIME:	2 minutes, 30 seconds
END CUE:	Shaun's voice-over says, "I did some heavy meditating."
DURATION:	1 minute, 15 seconds

Overview: Shaun's buddies convince him to ditch class and go surfing with them. Lonny hits the tsunamic surf, dying under a "righteous wave."

Illustration: Hundreds of sources constantly pressure us, but our friends hold the most swaying power. Christians can't allow the desire to fit in to overpower their integrity. Use this discussion to empower your youth to stand firm in the face of peer pressure.

Questions

- **What kinds of peer pressure do you experience?**
- **Why is it difficult to resist peer pressure?**
  Read aloud 1 Corinthians 15:33-34.
- **How much power do your friends have over you?**
- **How can you draw strength from God in the face of pressure?**
- **What lines do you need to draw for yourself about what you will and will not do, no matter what kind of pressure friends put on you?**

Perspective | THINGS ARE DIFFERENT FROM UP HERE

Title: DEAD POETS SOCIETY (PG)
Touchstone Pictures, 1989

Scripture: 2 Corinthians 1:3-7

Alternate Take: Scripture (Hebrews 4:12)

START TIME:	43 minutes, 00 seconds
START CUE:	Professor Keating leaps on top of his desk.
END TIME:	44 minutes, 15 seconds
END CUE:	The class moans at the assignment.
DURATION:	1 minute, 15 seconds

Overview: Professor Keating stands on his desk to gain a different perspective. He invites the entire class to stand on it, challenging them to constantly look at things from a different perspective.

Illustration: The ability to shift perspectives is a blessed talent that Christians should cultivate. By seeing the world through someone else's eyes, we can learn to empathize with people who desperately need God, instead of offering only condemnation.

Questions

- Have you ever changed your mind about an issue after gaining a new perspective? What happened?
- What stops people from gaining understanding by walking in someone else's shoes?

  Read aloud 2 Corinthians 1:3-7.

- How can gaining new perspectives help us show compassion to others?
- How can you learn to look at situations from different perspectives?

Possessions | DUST IN THE WIND

Title: THE NAKED GUN: FROM THE
FILES OF POLICE SQUAD! (PG-13)
Paramount Pictures, 1988

Scripture: Luke 12:16-23

Alternate Takes: Self-Worth (Deuteronomy 8:17-19),
Lying (Leviticus 19:11-12), Mistakes (Proverbs 28:13)

START TIME:	18 minutes, 15 seconds
START CUE:	Ludwig and Lt. Drebin shake hands.
END TIME:	21 minutes, 00 seconds
END CUE:	Lt. Drebin drops the fish back in the tank.
DURATION:	2 minutes, 45 seconds

Overview: Ludwig points out his priceless possessions to Lt. Drebin—a twenty thousand dollar fish and a rare samurai pen from Emperor Hirohito. Lt. Drebin accidentally tosses the pen into the fish tank, gets bit by the fish, then stabs the fish dead with the pen.

Illustration: This is the ultimate "D'oh!" It also shows how fleeting material possessions are. Help your youth see the temporal value of material things (especially before they have too many), encouraging them to make eternal things the "priceless" items in their lives.

Questions

- What are your most prized possessions?
- What makes them so precious to you, and how would you react if they were broken or stolen?

  Read aloud Luke 12:16-23.

- Are possessions bad? Why or why not?

- What kinds of things can be "stored" in heaven eternally?
- How can you shift to holding worldly possessions lightly and begin investing in the eternal?

Possibilities | IT CAN'T BE DONE

Title: OCEAN'S ELEVEN (PG-13)
Warner Bros., 2001

Scripture: Luke 18:27
Alternate Takes: Stealing (Exodus 20:15), Jericho (Joshua 6:1-16)

START TIME:	30 minutes, 30 seconds
START CUE:	Danny begins to present the plan.
END TIME:	33 minutes, 30 seconds
END CUE:	Saul swallows a pill.
DURATION:	3 minutes

Overview: Danny Ocean describes the impenetrable security system that protects the safes of the Bellagio, MGM Grand, and Mirage casinos in Las Vegas. His crew sits stunned at the prospect of trying to rob the impossible targets.

Illustration: Situations often look impossible from a human perspective. Yet everything suddenly becomes possible with God calling the shots! Use this illustration to challenge your students to let God fill in the gaps of their impossible tasks.

Questions
- What are some things from history that people once thought were impossible, but later were achieved?
  Read aloud Luke 18:27.
- Should a Christian ever label a situation impossible? Why or why not?
- Why does God often call his children to seemingly impossible tasks?
- How can you learn to use God's perspective instead of your own when you're assessing the "possibility" of a situation?

Themes L-Q

Title: THE FIFTH ELEMENT (PG-13)
Columbia Pictures, 1997

Scripture: Deuteronomy 8:17-19

Alternate Take: Mercy (Zechariah 7:9-10)

START TIME:	53 minutes, 45 seconds
START CUE:	Zorg asks, "What's wrong with me?"
END TIME:	56 minutes, 30 seconds
END CUE:	Zorg waves Priest Vito away.
DURATION:	2 minutes, 45 seconds

Overview: Zorg claims to encourage life since the destruction he brings makes life "interesting." Suddenly, Zorg chokes on a cherry. Priest Vito notes that Zorg's immense power is fleeting since it can all be toppled by a single cherry. Vito hits Zorg on the back and dislodges the cherry to prove his point.

Illustration: Many people in this world lust for and pursue power. Human power must seem funny to God, since any power accumulated on earth holds no heavenly weight and can disappear instantly. Present God's view of power with this clip, and discuss ways to use power for furthering God's kingdom instead of inflating a person's ego.

Questions

- **Who are the most powerful people in the world, and what would you do with their power if you had it?**
  Read aloud Deuteronomy 8:17-19.
- **Why does God allow corrupt people to be so powerful?**
- **Can a person be powerful without becoming corrupt? Why or why not?**
- **How can you prepare yourself now to use any power you gain wisely?**

Praise and Worship | MAKE A JOYFUL NOISE

Title: SISTER ACT (PG)
Touchstone Pictures, 1992

Scripture: Psalm 33:1-3

Alternate Take: Rejoice (Psalm 32:11)

START TIME:	30 minutes, 30 seconds
START CUE:	The church service starts.
END TIME:	32 minutes, 30 seconds
END CUE:	A nun performs the finale on the piano.
DURATION:	2 minutes

Overview: A choir of nuns completely butchers a song because of its horrible out-of-tune singing and lifeless attitude.

Illustration: People sometimes forget why we sing in church. Refresh participants' understanding of the purpose of singing praises and discuss ways to ignite a passion for worshipping God through song.

Questions
- **What are your favorite praise songs or hymns?**
  Read aloud Psalm 33:1-3.
- **Why do we sing songs to God?**
- **How can you tell the difference between simply singing and truly praising God?**
- **How can you learn to sing praises to God with all of your heart and soul?**

Prayer | NO ATHEISTS IN FOXHOLES

Title: O BROTHER, WHERE ART THOU? (PG-13)
Touchstone Pictures, 2000

Scripture: John 14:13-14
Alternate Takes: Mercy (Romans 9:15-16),
Injustice (Isaiah 59:14-16)

START TIME:	1 hour, 35 minutes, 00 seconds
START CUE:	Everett says, "You cain't do this!"
END TIME:	1 hour, 38 minutes, 00 seconds
END CUE:	A wall of water floods everything.
DURATION:	3 minutes

Overview: Everett, Delmar, and Pete—innocent men—stand before nooses, waiting to be hanged, and praying to God for mercy on their souls. Everett falls to his knees, pleading and confessing passionately to God. Suddenly, a rumble grows louder and louder, and a flood of water hits them all, answering their prayers.

Illustration: God answers prayer a million different ways, but he is *not* a cosmic Santa Claus. Many factors can shift our prayers away from communicating with God to a focus on self-centered topics. Use this scene to explore the purpose and passion behind prayer and to build teenagers' confidence in a caring God who always listens.

Questions
- What is the purpose of prayer?
- Have you ever prayed earnestly for something, but God didn't answer your prayer the way you wanted? What happened?

  Read aloud John 14:13-14.
- What are these verses really saying, since we know that people don't receive every single thing they ask of God?
- What role does patience play in prayer?

Preparation | I'M BORED

Title: BEHIND ENEMY LINES (PG-13)
20th Century Fox, 2001

Scripture: 1 Peter 5:8-9

Alternate Takes: Attitude (Philippians 3:12-16), Confrontation (Galatians 2:11)

START TIME:	9 minutes, 30 seconds
START CUE:	Burnett enters.
END TIME:	12 minutes, 15 seconds
END CUE:	Burnett exits.
DURATION:	2 minutes, 45 seconds

Overview: Reigart asks Burnett why he's leaving the Navy when he has so much wasted potential. Burnett says that the routine of pretending to be at war has drained him. Reigart claims that's what prepares a person for war.

Illustration: Prayer, attending church, and personal Bible study might seem repetitious, but they prepare us to face temptation and must be pursued diligently so we can avoid stumbling when trials arrive. Use this clip to prepare your troops for the spiritual war that rages around them.

Questions
- How do you prepare yourself for a test or competition?

  Read aloud 1 Peter 5:8-9.
- Why don't people prepare themselves spiritually?
- What are some methods for preparing yourself, and how can you integrate them into your life?
- How will greater spiritual preparation help you stand firm in your faith?

Pride | NEVER FEAR, I'M HERE

Title: RUSH HOUR (PG-13)
New Line Cinema, 1998

Scripture: Luke 14:7-11

Alternate Take: Humility (Micah 6:6-8)

START TIME:	17 minutes, 15 seconds
START CUE:	Carter enters the room.
END TIME:	19 minutes, 30 seconds
END CUE:	Carter says, "Yeah, I understand. You want me to baby-sit somebody... I came down here for the big assignment."
DURATION:	2 minutes, 30 seconds

> **Warning!** *A swear word is said soon after the End Cue for this clip, so make sure to stop the movie at the right time.*

Overview: Carter sweeps into the room, giving orders on how to run the investigation. Agent Russ puts the kibosh on Carter's plans by assigning him to baby-sit Officer Lee while the real pros work on solving the kidnapping.

Illustration: There's nothing like getting spanked after your pride precedes you. In Scripture, Jesus clearly explains the benefits of humility, so pass on the wisdom before foolish pride slaps someone in your group upside the head.

Questions

- **Have you ever been put in your place because of pride as Carter was? If so, what happened?**
- **What do you have the most pride about in your life, and how does that affect your actions toward others?**
  Read aloud Luke 14:7-11.
- **What motivates a person to take the best seat or the spotlight?**
- **Why does God detest pride?**
- **How can you learn to become more humble, and how would that affect your relationships?**

Themes I-Q

Title: DISNEY'S THE KID (PG)
Walt Disney Productions, 2000

Scripture: Galatians 5:16-25

Alternate Takes: Expectations (Luke 4:16-30),
Direction (Luke 6:47-49)

START TIME:	40 minutes, 15 seconds
START CUE:	Rusty looks for Chester.
END TIME:	42 minutes, 45 seconds
END CUE:	Rusty says, "I grow up to be a loser."
DURATION:	2 minutes, 30 seconds

Overview: Rusty calls out for his dog, Chester. Russell tells him there's no dog in the house. Rusty can't believe he grows up to be a single man with no dog, no plane, and no ability to pilot.

Illustration: Sometimes the busyness of life sidetracks us from what's really important. Keeping priorities straight only gets harder the older you get, so challenge your students to decide now about what's most important to them and commit to keeping first things first.

Questions

- What are the most important things in a person's life?
- What kinds of things distract people from these priorities?
  Read aloud Galatians 5:16-25.
- How are the priorities mentioned in this Scripture different from the priorities most people have?
- How can you keep your priorities in place over the next five, ten, and twenty years?

Profanity | &@#$*!&@$!

Title: A CHRISTMAS STORY (PG)
MGM, 1983

Scripture: Proverbs 10:31-32

Alternate Take: Punishment (Proverbs 13:24)

START TIME:	40 minutes, 00 seconds
START CUE:	Mom says, "Ralph, why don't you go help your father."
END TIME:	42 minutes, 45 seconds

END CUE:	Ralph thinks, "Lifebuoy, on the other hand..."
DURATION:	2 minutes, 45 seconds

Overview: Ralph helps his dad change a flat tire and says "fudge" when he accidentally drops the bolts.

Illustration: In a society that's developing increasingly "looser lips," it's difficult to keep a pure tongue. Challenge your young people to hold a high standard for their language by saying no to profanity.

Questions

- Why is profanity becoming more acceptable in our society?
- Do you think profanity is always wrong? Why or why not?
  Read aloud Proverbs 10:31-32.
- Why does God care if we use profanity or not?
- How can a person break the habit of using foul language?

Promises | YOU PROMISED!

Title: E.T. THE EXTRA-TERRESTRIAL (PG)
Universal Pictures, 1982

Scripture: Numbers 30:2

Alternate Take: Doubting Thomas (John 20:24-29)

START TIME:	32 minutes, 00 seconds
START CUE:	Elliot lets Michael into the room.
END TIME:	33 minutes, 30 seconds
END CUE:	Gertie enters and screams.
DURATION:	1 minute, 30 seconds

Overview: Elliot makes Michael swear not to tell about the goblin. Michael promises, not believing Elliot's story. Elliot brings out E.T., and Michael is flabbergasted.

Illustration: Unfortunately, a person's word isn't regarded as a bond. People break promises every day, especially when they don't take into account the consequences of saying yes. Use this scene to reinforce how serious making and keeping promises should be.

Questions

- Do people take promises seriously today? Why or why not?
- What makes a person think he or she can take a promise lightly?
  Read aloud Numbers 30:2.
- What does breaking a promise say to others? to God?
- What should you consider when making promises in the future?

Prophecy | I FORESEE GREAT THINGS

Title: O BROTHER, WHERE ART THOU? (PG-13)
Touchstone Pictures, 2000

Scripture: 1 Corinthians 12:28-31
Alternate Takes: Isaiah (2 Kings 20:2-7),
Hearing God (Matthew 11:12-15)

START TIME:	6 minutes, 30 seconds
START CUE:	Everett says, "Mind if we join you?"
END TIME:	8 minutes, 30 seconds
END CUE:	The handcar rides into the sunset.
DURATION:	2 minutes

Overview: A blind man manually pumps a handcar along the railroad tracks. The guys hop on for a ride. The blind man suddenly spouts off several obtuse prophecies about their future.

Illustration: The Bible brims with prophecy, some already fulfilled and some still pending. It's an area many overlook, misuse, or misunderstand. Clear the confusion by explaining prophecy—its use in the Bible and how God uses it today.

Questions

- **What are some biblical prophecies that have been fulfilled? What are some that haven't?**
- **Since prophecy is sometimes difficult to understand and believe, what's God's purpose for prophecy?**
  Read aloud 1 Corinthians 12:28-31.
- **Does God use prophecy today? If so, how?**
- **How can you discern whether a prophecy is true or not?**

Punishment | I DON'T DESERVE THIS

Title: SUPERMAN (PG)
Warner Bros., 1978

Scripture: Hebrews 12:5-11
Alternate Takes: Judgment (Ecclesiastes 3:15-17),
Lucifer (Isaiah 14:12-15)

START TIME:	6 minutes, 45 seconds
START CUE:	Jor-El presents the indictments.
END TIME:	9 minutes, 45 seconds
END CUE:	General Zod looks up.
DURATION:	3 minutes

Overview: Jor-El prosecutes General Zod, Ursa, and Non for heinous crimes against Krypton. The council pronounces them guilty. Zod claims with pride that they will all bow before him some day.

Illustration: There's a time to forgive and a time to punish. Understanding the why and when of this biblical principle can take some doing. Help teenagers look at God's judgment through Scripture, discover his heart on the matter, and find ways to apply his pattern of discipline and forgiveness in daily life.

Questions
- **How did your parents punish you when you were a child?**
- **Do you think their punishments were fair? Why or why not?**
  Read aloud Hebrews 12:5-11.
- **If God is love, why does he punish people?**
- **How does God decide when to offer grace and when to punish?**

Purpose | YOU'RE HERE FOR A REASON

Title: SUPERMAN (PG)
Warner Bros., 1978

Scripture: Jeremiah 29:11
Alternate Take: Humility (James 4:10)

START TIME:	30 minutes, 00 seconds
START CUE:	Clark runs alongside a train.
END TIME:	33 minutes, 00 seconds
END CUE:	Clark says, "Thanks, Dad."
DURATION:	3 minutes

Overview: Clark runs faster than a speeding train to beat some classmates in a car. Pa chastises Clark for showing off. Clark asks if it's wrong to do the things you were made to do. Pa says it's not, but emphasizes that Clark was put on earth for a reason that's far larger than scoring touchdowns.

Illustration: God has a purpose for everyone, but what is it? Help your young people find their gifts and talents and discover the purpose God has for them in building his kingdom.

Questions

- **What do you think your purpose is here on earth?**
  Read aloud Jeremiah 29:11.
- **How does knowing that God has a plan for you make you feel?**
- **Since God has a plan for you, why doesn't he come right out and tell you exactly what it is?**
- **How can you figure out what God's plan is for your life?**

Questions | I DON'T GET IT

Title: BIG (PG)
20th Century Fox, 1988

Scripture: Acts 17:10-12

Alternate Takes: Seeking Answers (Jeremiah 33:2-3),
Wisdom (Proverbs 19:20)

START TIME:	42 minutes, 30 seconds
START CUE:	An office meeting begins.
END TIME:	45 minutes, 15 seconds
END CUE:	MacMillan says, "Well done, Josh. Well done."
DURATION:	2 minutes, 45 seconds

Overview: Josh plays with a robot toy during a meeting. He doesn't understand what's supposed to make the toy fun. Paul provides marketing statistics but not an answer for what makes it fun. Josh still doesn't understand and suggests a different toy idea.

Illustration: Sometimes we're embarrassed to ask questions in church or to ask questions of God. It seems as if everyone's supposed to know all the answers, but life with God can be confusing. Use this scene to help students realize that asking questions actually helps faith grow.

Questions

- **Why do people sometimes feel uncomfortable with asking questions in a church setting?**
- **Does God welcome questions? Why or why not?**
  Read aloud Acts 17:10-12.
- **How did asking questions help the Bereans grow in faith?**
- **What are some questions you've always wanted to ask about God or faith?**

Racism | DIFFERENT WRAPPERS

Title: REMEMBER THE TITANS (PG)
Walt Disney Productions, 2000

Scripture: Colossians 3:9-11

Alternate Takes: Respect (Matthew 21:33-39),
War (Nahum 3:1-3)

START TIME:	32 minutes, 00 seconds
START CUE:	The team enters a clearing.
END TIME:	34 minutes, 00 seconds
END CUE:	Coach Boone says, "Maybe we'll learn to play this game like men."
DURATION:	2 minutes

Overview: The team finishes their run at the battlefield of Gettysburg. Coach
Boone tells them how fifty thousand men died fighting the same racial battles
that they face today.

Illustration: Like Coach Boone reminds the boys, we're still fighting some of these
same racial battles today. God is the great healer who can bring his children
together in harmony and unity. Use this discussion to destroy any racial stereotypes or divisions among your teenagers and discuss practical ways to bring
healing to your community.

Questions
- **What causes people to have racist attitudes?**
- **How have you seen people affected by racism?**
  Read aloud Colossians 3:9-11.
- **What makes racism so destructive?**
- **How can someone learn to see others as equals?**
- **How can you combat racism?**

Reconciliation | JUST CALL HIM

Title: HOME ALONE (PG)
20th Century Fox, 1990

Scripture: Matthew 5:23-26

Alternate Takes: Rumors (Jeremiah 51:46),
Family (Deuteronomy 5:16), Fear (Psalm 91:1-6)

START TIME:	1 hour, 8 minutes, 45 seconds
START CUE:	Old Man Marley sits down next to Kevin.
END TIME:	1 hour, 11 minutes, 45 seconds
END CUE:	Kevin says, "I'd talk to my dad."
DURATION:	3 minutes

Overview: Kevin admits he said bad things about his family. Old Man Marley says families love each other deep down, even though they hurt each other. He explains that he still loves his son, even though they never reconciled after a fight. Kevin encourages Old Man Marley to face his fear and call his son.

Illustration: "I'm sorry" might be the hardest phrase we ever utter. The path toward healing in relationships, though, passes through reconciliation. Use this clip to tout the benefits of reconciliation by exploring methods for navigating its frightening path.

Questions

- **Do you have any unresolved disputes with friends or family members? If so, what are they?**
- **What factors make it difficult to reconcile with someone?**
  Read aloud Matthew 5:23-26.
- **What happens to us both emotionally and spiritually when we don't reconcile with others?**
- **What are the benefits to reconciling with others?**

Refuge | THE STORMS OF LIFE

Title: TWISTER (PG-13)
Warner Bros., 1996

Scripture: Deuteronomy 33:26-29

Alternate Take: Trials (Deuteronomy 7:17-21)

START TIME:	31 minutes, 45 seconds
START CUE:	The truck slams into a small bridge.
END TIME:	33 minutes, 45 seconds
END CUE:	The truck lands on the highway.
DURATION:	2 minutes

Overview: Bill and Jo's truck slams into a bridge. They jump out and hide under the bridge. The tornado passes over them, sucking their truck up with it, but leaving the couple alive.

Illustration: Everyone has a storm pass through their life at times, damaging everything in its path. Use this scene to show how important it is to seek God as the perfect refuge during these times of trial.

Questions

- Where are some places people go in order to seek safety?
- What happens when a person's place of refuge doesn't withstand the storm? Read aloud Deuteronomy 33:26-29.
- If God is a refuge, why do bad things still happen?
- How can a person feel safe finding refuge in an invisible God?

Regeneration | I FEEL SO ALIVE

Title: HOOP DREAMS (PG-13)
Fine Line Features, 1994

Scripture: John 1:12-13
Alternate Takes: Drugs (Philippians 3:17-19), Forgiveness (Isaiah 55:6-7)

START TIME:	1 hour, 9 minutes, 45 seconds
START CUE:	The Agee family walks to church.
END TIME:	1 hour, 11 minutes, 45 seconds
END CUE:	The church door is shown.
DURATION:	2 minutes, 00 seconds

Overview: Mr. Agee returns to the family after serving jail time for drugs. He sings a testimony of redemption and shares how God gave him new life and forgiveness in jail.

Illustration: Only God's grace can regenerate the most desperate of sinners (including you and me). The change that can occur overnight when a person surrenders his or her life and pride to Jesus is amazing. Bring the complex religious term *regeneration* to life with this clip.

Questions

- Has anyone you've known ever seemed to change overnight? What happened? Read aloud John 1:12-13.
- How does becoming a child of God bring regeneration to a person's life?
- Should a person who repents immediately change? Why or why not?
- What areas of your life has God regenerated, and what areas need to be?

Reincarnation | I WAS CLEOPATRA!

Title: THE MUMMY RETURNS (PG-13)
Universal Pictures, 2001

Scripture: Job 14:5-12

Alternate Take: Destiny (Romans 8:28-30)

START TIME:	1 hour, 12 minutes, 30 seconds
START CUE:	Rick says, "Evie, I know you haven't exactly been yourself lately."
END TIME:	1 hour, 13 minutes, 15 seconds
END CUE:	Ardeth says, "There is a fine line between coincidence and fate."
DURATION:	45 seconds

Overview: Evie experiences flashes of memory from a previous life. Ardeth insists that Rick is destined to protect Evie, that everyone's life journey is written. Rick blows it off as coincidence, but Ardeth states that there's a fine line between coincidence and fate.

Illustration: More and more people buy into the reincarnation craze every day. The Bible is very clear that we only get one trip on spaceship Earth. Use this discussion to root out any misunderstanding among your young people regarding what happens when they die.

Questions
- **What do you think about reincarnation?**
- **Why would a person want to be reincarnated?**
  Read aloud Job 14:5-12.
- **Why does God limit the number of our days on earth?**
- **How can you make each day you have on earth count for eternity?**

Rejection | CRUSHED HEART ON SLEEVE

Title: RIDING IN CARS WITH BOYS (PG-13)
Columbia Pictures, 2001

Scripture: Isaiah 40:28-31

Alternate Take: Fear (Isaiah 54:4)

START TIME:	14 minutes, 45 seconds
START CUE:	Bev says, "Listen, I'm doing something incredibly daring right now..."
END TIME:	16 minutes, 00 seconds
END CUE:	Bev runs away.
DURATION:	1 minute, 15 seconds

Overview: Bev works up the courage to approach Sky. Tommy says the hero and coward have one thing in common—fear. He says that being scared doesn't make her a coward. Bev gives Sky the note. He reads it aloud and ridicules her in front of everyone.

Illustration: Everyone tastes rejection at some point—and it's always bitter. Rejection can take many forms (romantic, social, and familial, for example) but God can offer us healing in the midst of these painful experiences.

Questions

- **Have you ever felt rejected? What happened?**
- **What makes rejection so painful?**
  Read aloud Isaiah 40:28-31.
- **Why does God care about people who are rejected?**
- **How can God comfort your feelings of rejection and give you the strength to carry on?**

Reverence | THAT'S NOT A TOY!

Title: UNBREAKABLE (PG-13)
Touchstone Pictures, 2000

Scripture: Matthew 7:6
Alternate Take: Spiritual Treasures (Matthew 6:20-21)

START TIME:	25 minutes, 00 seconds
START CUE:	A comic book sketch fills the screen.
END TIME:	27 minutes, 15 seconds
END CUE:	Elijah says, "This is a piece of art."
DURATION:	2 minutes, 15 seconds

Overview: Elijah shows an "art" piece (a rare comic book sketch) to a potential buyer. The man agrees to buy it, excited about giving it to his four-year-old son. Elijah snaps, refusing to sell the piece because he runs an art gallery, not a toy store.

Illustration: We treat the things of God so flippantly sometimes. Yes, God is our closest friend and confidant, but he's also the supreme ruler and creator of the entire universe. Use this clip to promote a proper reverence for God, his Word, and his church.

Questions

- **Do people show God as much reverence as Elijah shows his comic books? Why or why not?**
  Read aloud Matthew 7:6.

- **What are some spiritual things that people treat flippantly?**
- **Why do people often lose reverence for God, the Bible, and the church?**
- **How can you show more reverence for the things of God?**

Romantic Love | HAPPILY EVER AFTER

Title: THE NAKED GUN: FROM THE FILES OF POLICE SQUAD! (PG-13)
Paramount Pictures, 1988

Scripture: 1 Corinthians 13

Alternate Take: Dating (Proverbs 4:23)

START TIME:	41 minutes, 15 seconds
START CUE:	Lt. Drebin and Jane run through the surf.
END TIME:	42 minutes, 30 seconds
END CUE:	Lt. Drebin and Jane "clothesline" some people.
DURATION:	1 minute, 15 seconds

Overview: Lt. Drebin and Jane frolic, in love.

Illustration: This hypervision of love isn't far from what the media typically feeds people. Help your youth understand what romantic love really is and how to discern the real thing from fleeting hormone rushes and bouts of lust.

Questions
- **How does it feel when you first start dating someone?**
- **What can make those feelings change?**
  Read aloud 1 Corinthians 13.
- **How is this description of love different from what you see and hear in movies and music?**
- **Where does romance fit inside God's definition of love?**
- **How can someone discern the difference between real love and infatuation or lust?**

Rules | THEY'RE MADE TO BREAK

Title: HOME ALONE (PG)
20th Century Fox, 1990

Scripture: Psalm 119:95-105

Alternate Takes: Freedom (2 Corinthians 3:17-18),
Obedience (Romans 6:16-18)

START TIME:	22 minutes, 00 seconds
START CUE:	Kevin jumps on the bed.
END TIME:	23 minutes, 30 seconds
END CUE:	Kevin shoots the door closed.
DURATION:	1 minute, 15 seconds

Overview: Kevin goes wild, doing everything that's forbidden in the house like running, jumping on beds, and shooting his BB gun.

Illustration: A lot of people perceive God as the cosmic killjoy, and they think the Bible is full of rules to ruin the party. In reality, obeying God produces true freedom. Destroy the bad rap that God's rules get by explaining the loving reasons behind them.

Questions

- **What rule did you hate growing up?**
- **Why was that rule in place?**
  Read aloud Psalm 119:95-105.
- **Is it weird to "love" God's rules? Why or why not?**
- **Why do people think God's rules prevent fun?**
- **What are the benefits of following God's rules?**

The Sabbath | TAKE A LOAD OFF

Title: CHARIOTS OF FIRE (PG)
Warner Bros., 1981

Scripture: Exodus 20:8-11

Alternate Take: Peer Pressure (Deuteronomy 13:6-8)

START TIME:	1 hour, 27 minutes, 15 seconds
START CUE:	Liddell meets the Duke of Sutherland.
END TIME:	1 hour, 30 minutes, 15 seconds
END CUE:	Liddell says, "God knows I love my country, but I can't make that sacrifice."
DURATION:	3 minutes

Overview: Eric Liddell refuses to run on Sunday because it's the Sabbath. Men representing England pressure him into running, saying that he must place his country before God. Liddell counters that God made countries in the first place.

Illustration: Even though we often don't take the Sabbath very seriously, God does. Scripture clearly states numerous times that we are to relax and reflect on him one day of each week. Challenge your youth to dedicate one day every week to God and see how God miraculously rewards them.

Questions

- Do you rest on the Sabbath? Why or why not?
  Read aloud Exodus 20:8-11.
- What is God's intent with this command and what makes an activity "work"?
- What are the benefits of keeping the Sabbath?
- How can you arrange your life this week so you can truly take a Sabbath?

Sacrifice | STEPPING IN FRONT

Title: THE IRON GIANT (PG)
Warner Bros., 1999

Scripture: John 15:12-13

Alternate Take: Enemies (Matthew 5:43-48)

START TIME:	1 hour, 14 minutes, 00 seconds
START CUE:	Hogarth gets out of the Iron Giant's hand.
END TIME:	1 hour, 16 minutes, 30 seconds
END CUE:	The general says, "Let's go home."
DURATION:	2 minutes, 30 seconds

Overview: The Iron Giant, feared and attacked by the humans, saves his enemies by intercepting a nuclear missile and getting blown up.

Illustration: Every guy I know cries at this part of the movie. It's not only because every dude wants a robot, but also because the Iron Giant's sacrifice for people who both loved and hated him embodies such truth and honor. In a world that looks out for number one, genuine sacrifice grabs people's immediate attention.

Questions

- Who are some people who've sacrificed something for you, and what did they do?
  Read aloud John 15:12-13.
- What are some ways to lay down your life for someone besides physically dying?

- **What prevents people from sacrificing for those around them?**
- **How can you sacrifice for someone else this week?**

Samuel | WHO SAID THAT?

Title: FIELD OF DREAMS (PG)
Universal Pictures, 1989

Scripture: 1 Samuel 3:1-10

Alternate Takes: Hearing God (Psalm 81:8), Faith (John 20:24-29)

START TIME:	4 minutes, 15 seconds
START CUE:	Ray walks in his cornfield.
END TIME:	5 minutes, 45 seconds
END CUE:	Ray leaves the cornfield.
DURATION:	1 minute, 30 seconds

Overview: Ray hears a voice say, "If you build it, he will come," and Ray tries to find out who's talking.

Illustration: Samuel felt this way when God came calling. Use this scene to discuss what God's voice "sounds like" so those in your ministry can recognize his call.

Questions

Read aloud 1 Samuel 3:1-10.
- **Does God speak to people this way any more? Explain.**
- **Has God ever spoken to you? If so, what happened?**
- **What are some ways God chooses to speak to people?**
- **How do you discern whether it's really God talking or not?**

Science | WE KILLED GOD!

Title: THE 6TH DAY (PG-13)
Columbia Pictures, 2000

Scripture: Job 38

Alternate Takes: Death (Deuteronomy 32:39),
God's Sovereignty (1 Chronicles 29:11-13)

Themes **R-Z**

START TIME:	1 hour, 30 minutes, 15 seconds
START CUE:	Adam says, "I know who I am."
END TIME:	1 hour, 33 minutes, 15 seconds
END CUE:	Drucker says, "I'm just taking over where God left off."
DURATION:	3 minutes

Warning! *A swear word is said soon after the End Cue for this clip, so make sure to stop the movie at the right time.*

Overview: Drucker claims to have the ability to conquer death. Adam counters that only God has the right to decide who deserves to live and die. Drucker laughs, explaining that even if God existed, he gave humans the ability to understand science and use it to move civilization forward.

Illustration: There will always be tension between faith and science. Help teenagers explore how their faith can inform their understanding of science instead of just contradicting it. God did give us the mental faculties to make amazing discoveries, but nothing we achieve will ever replace our need for the loving creator.

Questions
- Do you think science is inherently evil? Why or why not?
- What are some things you learn at school that seem to contradict God's Word?
- How do you reconcile these things with your faith?
  Read aloud Job 38.
- What are some things science can't explain that the Bible can?
- How does believing in an almighty Creator help you when you study science?

Scripture | IT'S IN THERE SOMEWHERE

Title: DR. SUESS' HOW THE GRINCH
STOLE CHRISTMAS (PG)
Universal Pictures, 2000

Scripture: Psalm 119:127-133

Alternate Takes: Kindness (Proverbs 14:20-21),
Abuse of Power (Job 21:7-9)

START TIME:	34 minutes, 00 seconds
START CUE:	The mayor steps up to the podium.
END TIME:	36 minutes, 15 seconds
END CUE:	The crowd claps in agreement.
DURATION:	2 minutes, 15 seconds

Overview: The crowd makes nominations for the Whoville Holiday Cheermeister. Cindy nominates the Grinch because he needs it most and the Book of Who doesn't forbid it. Mayor Maywho obviously makes up a verse saying the Grinch can't be the Cheermeister.

Illustration: Nothing has been used and abused for personal gain as much as God's Word. That's what makes knowing Scripture so important—so we can discern right from wrong both in our own lives and in the teachings of others. Challenge participants to learn Scripture and take it to heart for the protection of themselves and others.

Questions

- **What are some facts and phrases people think are in the Bible that really aren't?**
- **How important is memorizing Scripture?**
  Read aloud Psalm 119:127-133.
- **How can knowing Scripture protect you?**
- **What are some practical ways you can make Scripture a part of your daily life?**

Second Chances | I'M UP FOR PAROLE

Title: MYSTERY MEN (PG-13)
Universal Pictures, 1999

Scripture: Micah 7:7-9

Alternate Takes: Forgiveness (1 John 1:8-10), Compassion (Hebrews 13:1-3), Justice (Isaiah 56:1-2)

START TIME:	13 minutes, 00 seconds
START CUE:	Lance Hunt enters the room and asks, "Am I too late to cast my vote?"
END TIME:	14 minutes, 30 seconds
END CUE:	Casanova gets parole.
DURATION:	1 minute, 30 seconds

Overview: The parole board rejects Casanova Frankenstein's bid for release. Lance Hunt brings Captain Amazing's request that the board show compassion in the face of justice.

Illustration: Everyone needs a second chance. While it's hard for us to balance justice and compassion, every human being needs the spiritual second chance that God offers. Use this scene to illustrate how our "heavenly attorney," Jesus, pleads our case for parole from eternal separation from God.

Questions

- Is it difficult to get a second chance in life? Why or why not?
- Why does every human being need a second chance spiritually?
  Read aloud Micah 7:7-9.
- Why does God plead our case for us even though we're guilty?
- How can we extend second chances to others as God has to us?

Self-Control | I'M IN TRAINING

Title: ROCKY (PG)
United Artists, 1976

Scripture: 1 Corinthians 9:24-27

Alternate Takes: Preparation (Matthew 26:37-41),
Perseverance (James 1:2-4)

START TIME:	1 hour, 30 minutes, 30 seconds
START CUE:	Rocky starts jogging.
END TIME:	1 hour, 33 minutes, 00 seconds
END CUE:	Rocky stands in victory at the top of the steps.
DURATION:	2 minutes, 30 seconds

Overview: Rocky trains diligently using running, punching, and other methods of physical training.

Illustration: Working hard to control the body can play a big part in one's spiritual maturity. Use this clip to challenge participants to gain mastery of their bodies so they can "get the prize."

Questions

- How does training help an athlete control his or her body?
- In which areas of life do you have self-control? Where are you weak?
  Read aloud 1 Corinthians 9:24-27.
- Why is it important to build self-control?
- What spiritual disciplines can help build self-control?
- How can you build self-control in weak areas of your life?

Self-Image | I'M REALLY A STUNT MAN

Title: MYSTERY MEN (PG-13)
Universal Pictures, 1999

Scripture: Psalm 139:13-16

Alternate Takes: Approval (John 12:42-43),
Lying (Ephesians 4:25)

START TIME:	1 hour, 28 minutes, 15 seconds
START CUE:	Monica comes down the stairs of her apartment building.
END TIME:	1 hour, 30 minutes, 15 seconds
END CUE:	Monica says, "Just be Roy."
DURATION:	2 minutes

Overview: Monica asks Mr. Furious for his real name. He tries to come up with an impressive story. She turns to leave, obviously bummed by his posturing, and he finally confesses, "It's Roy." She kisses him and encourages him to "just be Roy."

Illustration: Whether it's in dating, making friends, or just trying to fit in, people constantly try to impress others. God wants you to be content with being the best *you* can be. Use this discussion to encourage teenagers to be real and honest instead of seeking others' approval or pretending to be someone else.

Questions

- **Have you ever pretended to be something you're not in order to impress someone? What happened?**

   Read aloud Psalm 139:13-16.

- **Do you think you are wonderfully made? Why or why not?**
- **How can just being yourself glorify God?**
- **How can you improve your self-image this week and become more content?**

Selfishness | SERVE ME, PRONTO!

Title: THE EMPEROR'S NEW GROOVE (G)
Walt Disney Productions, 2000

Scripture: 2 Corinthians 5:14-15

Alternate Takes: Materialism (Ecclesiastes 2:4-11),
Enemies (Proverbs 25:21-22), Blame (Genesis 3:1-13)

START TIME:	31 minutes, 45 seconds
START CUE:	Kuzco orders Pacha around.
END TIME:	34 minutes, 00 seconds
END CUE:	Pacha covers Kuzco with his coat.
DURATION:	2 minutes, 15 seconds

Overview: Kuzco needs to be transformed back from a llama into a prince so that he can finally build Kuztopia. Pacha pleads with Kuzco to change his mind and warns Kuzco that he'll end up all alone because he only thinks about himself.

Illustration: Some people are completely shocked to discover that the world revolves around the sun, not them! While selfishness rules on every street corner, God calls his people to lay down their lives for others and leave "looking out for number one" behind.

Questions

- When was the last time you saw someone being selfish? What happened?
- What attitudes form the roots of selfishness?

Read aloud 2 Corinthians 5:14-15.

- How does God free people from selfishness?
- In which area of life are you selfish, and how can you change that?

Sex | I'M PREGNANT!

Title: RIDING IN CARS WITH BOYS (PG-13)
Columbia Pictures, 2001

Scripture: 1 Corinthians 6:15-20

Alternate Takes: Consequences (Genesis 3:9-24), Confession (James 5:16)

START TIME:	25 minutes, 45 seconds
START CUE:	Bev says, "I wanna be dead!"
END TIME:	27 minutes, 00 seconds
END CUE:	Fay says, "Maybe you should tell Ray first."
DURATION:	1 minute, 15 seconds

Overview: Bev freaks out because she's pregnant. Fay suggests it might help if she practices telling her parents the news. Bev confesses, and Fay rants at Bev like a parent, shouting, "My daughter's a tramp!"

Illustration: This is only one of the consequences of sex outside of marriage, along with emotional scars, STDs, and guilt. Use this clip to acknowledge the joy of sex within the boundaries of marriage while explaining the emotional, spiritual, and physical cost of stepping outside of God's guidelines.

Questions
- What things make sex a wonderful gift?
- What factors can make sex terrible?

  Read aloud 1 Corinthians 6:15-20.
- Why is sex outside of marriage so damaging?
- How can you deal with sexual urges in a moral way?

Sexism | YOU THROW LIKE A GIRL

Title: A LEAGUE OF THEIR OWN (PG)
Columbia Pictures, 1992

Scripture: Galatians 3:26-28

Alternate Take: Revenge (Leviticus 19:18)

START TIME:	37 minutes, 45 seconds
START CUE:	A spectator says, "Girls can't play ball."
END TIME:	38 minutes, 15 seconds
END CUE:	Blondie says, "It slipped."
DURATION:	30 seconds

Overview: A guy in the stands makes sexist remarks about the women on the ball field. The shortstop "accidentally" nails him with the baseball.

Illustration: Though women prove time and again that they are equal (or, like my wife, *better*), they still get knocked for being the "fairer" sex. Use this discussion to reveal how Jesus opened the door for women's rights and explore ways to help female participants find their rightful place in a "man's world."

Questions
- What are some sexist things you've heard people say?
- When and where have you seen sexism in your everyday life?

  Read aloud Galatians 3:26-28.
- Why is there neither "male nor female" when we also know that God made men and women different?
- How can you acknowledge the differences between the sexes without adopting sexist or superior attitudes?

Title: IN & OUT (PG-13)
Paramount Pictures, 1997

Scripture: Romans 1:26-27

Alternate Takes: Stereotypes (John 7:24),
Media Messages (Isaiah 32:1-8)

START TIME:	9 minutes, 30 seconds
START CUE:	The movie clip for "To Serve and Protect" starts.
END TIME:	12 minutes, 30 seconds
END CUE:	The screen says "The End."
DURATION:	3 minutes

Overview: Scenes from the movie "To Serve and Protect" play, depicting a gay soldier saving the injured soldier he loves, getting court-martialed, and then living as a homeless person with the man he loves.

Illustration: This fake film is pretty over the top, but should loosen people up enough to discuss a tough topic: sexuality. The Bible's very clear on this issue, but society often doesn't accept what it perceives as harsh or intolerant. Discuss sexuality with participants and explore ways to speak the truth with love and compassion, not venom.

Questions

- **Why do you think so many people today are confused about sexuality?** Read aloud Romans 1:26-27.
- **Why did God make sexual relations between men and women the "natural" function?**
- **What are the root causes of sexual confusion?**
- **How can we show love and compassion to people who struggle with their sexuality or whose views on sexuality differ from our own?**

Sharing Faith | **I'M GOING IN**

Title: THE PERFECT STORM (PG-13)
Warner Bros., 2000

Scripture: Jude 7-13

Alternate Takes: Sacrifice (Acts 20:22-24),
Courage (1 Samuel 17:32-37)

START TIME:	1 hour, 47 minutes, 30 seconds
START CUE:	The men swim for the boat.
END TIME:	1 hour, 50 minutes, 00 seconds
END CUE:	The crew drags the men on board.
DURATION:	2 minutes, 30 seconds

Overview: A man swims to a boat, dragging his incapacitated friend, but is unable to haul him on board. He refuses to let his friend die, though, and risks his life by jumping from the safety of the boat's deck back into the water to save him.

Illustration: People "drown" around us every day in a spiritual storm they can't even see. We can't *make* someone follow Christ, but we can jump in and live with urgency about the invisible danger. While it's easier to go out on a limb for someone in physical peril (because we can see it), we must begin looking with God's eyes at the spiritual jeopardy surrounding us.

Questions
- Would you jump in the water after a friend as the guy did in the clip? Why or why not?
- Would you do it for a stranger? Why or why not?
- Do you think people who don't know Jesus are in danger? Why or why not? Read aloud Jude 7-13.
- What is our responsibility to those ruled by their instincts instead of by God?
- What prevents you from telling your friends about salvation?

Sin | WHAT'S THE WORST THING YOU'VE DONE?

Title: SMOKE SIGNALS (PG-13)
Miramax Films, 1998

Scripture: Romans 8:1-4

Alternate Takes: Integrity (Proverbs 15:9-10), Evil (Matthew 15:17-20)

START TIME:	49 minutes, 45 seconds
START CUE:	Arnold and Suzy walk home.
END TIME:	51 minutes, 45 seconds
END CUE:	Arnold and Suzy walk in silence.
DURATION:	2 minutes, 00 seconds

Overview: Arnold asks, "What's the most evil thing you've ever done to another person?" Suzy answers that she once stole an old woman's purse and spent all of the money. Arnold presses her, and Suzy reluctantly admits she slept with her best friend's boyfriend. Arnold nods, "That's bad."

Illustration: There's no scale of sin in God's eyes, but our failures definitely have different levels of fallout. Some consequences leave deeper marks than others. Use this discussion to reiterate that God's grace can cover any sin but that people may not be so willing to forgive and forget.

Questions
- **What's the worst thing you've ever done? Why did you do it?**
- **What are the worst sins people can commit?**
  Read aloud Romans 8:1-4.
- **How can Jesus wipe away all sin? Explain.**
- **How can a person walk in the Spirit, free from sin and condemnation?**

Sin of Omission | IT'S TOO LATE NOW

Title: INDEPENDENCE DAY (PG-13)
20th Century Fox, 1996

Scripture: James 4:17

Alternate Take: Confrontation (Galatians 2:11-16)

START TIME:	1 hour, 4 minutes, 15 seconds
START CUE:	David exits the bathroom.
END TIME:	1 hour, 6 minutes, 15 seconds
END CUE:	David asks, "Which part?"
DURATION:	2 minutes

Overview: The president and his advisers discuss the possibility of nuclear attack against the aliens. Julius blames the government for not seizing its chance against the aliens with the spaceship at Area 51. The President swears there's no such thing. Nimzicki corrects the president, saying, "That's not entirely accurate."

Illustration: When we know we're supposed to do something, but we don't do it, people suffer. Use this scene to challenge your young people to seize opportunities to do what is right.

Questions
- **What happens when you don't do something you know you should?**
- **What factors keep you from doing the right thing?**
  Read aloud James 4:17.
- **What are some things you overlook in your life?**
- **How can you start doing what you know is right?**

The Soul | HOW MUCH IS THIS WORTH?

Title: O BROTHER, WHERE ART THOU? (PG-13)
Touchstone Pictures, 2000

Scripture: 2 Corinthians 5:1-10
Alternate Take: The Devil (Revelation 12:7-9)

START TIME:	21 minutes, 45 seconds
START CUE:	Tommy introduces himself.
END TIME:	23 minutes, 00 seconds
END CUE:	Everett asks, "How much he pay?"
DURATION:	1 minute, 15 seconds

Overview: The guys pick up Tommy, who reveals he just sold his soul to the devil in order to play the guitar. He claims it's no big deal since he wasn't using his soul.

Illustration: While most people use the word *soul* to describe James Brown, it's actually the part of us that separates humanity from the rest of creation. Use this clip to explain exactly what the soul is and why it's so important to our lives.

Questions

- **What do you think makes up a person's soul?**
  Read aloud 2 Corinthians 5:1-10.
- **What creates tension between our soul and our body?**
- **What kinds of things cause a person's soul to "groan"?**
- **What can you do to nurture and strengthen your soul?**

Speech | FOOLS REMOVE DOUBT

Title: BEST IN SHOW (PG-13)
Warner Bros., 2000

Scripture: Proverbs 15:1-2
Alternate Takes: Biblical Knowledge (Matthew 4:1-11),
Pride (Proverbs 14:12)

START TIME:	1 hour, 2 minutes, 00 seconds
START CUE:	Buck says, "We're here with Dr. Millbank."
END TIME:	1 hour, 3 minutes, 00 seconds
END CUE:	Dr. Millbank says, "It doesn't matter."
DURATION:	1 minute

Overview: Buck interviews Dr. Millbank and spouts out incredibly inaccurate historical information about Columbus and the Mayflower.

Illustration: It's usually a smart idea for a person to avoid speaking with authority or conviction when he or she doesn't have any knowledge on the topic. In a society filled with know-it-alls, people who are slow to speak stand out as reflections of the Spirit of God.

Questions

- **Who around you is a know-it-all, and how do people react toward that person?**
  Read aloud Proverbs 15:1-2.
- **What makes a person who speaks without thinking a fool?**
- **How does our speech impact how people view us? view Jesus?**
- **How can you learn to be more cautious when you speak?**

Spiritual Armor | STRAP IT ON

Title: TOMORROW NEVER DIES (PG-13)
MGM, 1997

Scripture: Ephesians 6:10-18

Alternate Take: Humility (Luke 18:11-14)

START TIME:	28 minutes, 45 seconds
START CUE:	A crate falls open to reveal a BMW.
END TIME:	30 minutes, 30 seconds
END CUE:	Q says, "Grow up, 007."
DURATION:	1 minute, 45 seconds

Overview: Q explains the specs on James Bond's new car and phone, equipping him for a new mission.

Illustration: James Bond never enters the field without getting all the necessary gear—and neither should we. Use this discussion to teach the importance of donning the armor of God and explain how each piece of spiritual equipment provides protection.

Questions

- **Why does James Bond always gear up before a mission?**
  Read aloud Ephesians 6:10-18.
- **Do you consistently gear up spiritually before leaving the house? Why or why not?**
- **What makes each piece of spiritual armor important?**
- **Which pieces do you typically forget to wear? Why?**
- **What prevents you from donning the full armor of God, and how can you learn to put everything on?**

Spiritual Blindness | I CAN SEE!

Drama

Title: AT FIRST SIGHT (PG-13)
MGM, 1999

Scripture: Isaiah 35:3-5

Alternate Takes: Discipleship (Proverbs 16:20-23),
New Life (2 Corinthians 5:17), Paul and Ananias (Acts 9:17-19)

START TIME:	53 minutes, 45 seconds
START CUE:	Dr. Aaron unwraps Virgil's head.
END TIME:	56 minutes, 45 seconds
END CUE:	Dr. Aaron says, "Give your eyes a rest."
DURATION:	3 minutes

Overview: Dr. Aaron removes the patches that cover Virgil's blinded eyes. Virgil opens his eyes, hoping to see for the very first time. He can't comprehend what the flashes of light and distorted shapes could be. Virgil freaks out until the doctor has him hold a Coke can so he can mentally associate his sense of touch with his newfound sight.

Illustration: Satan keeps people spiritually blind as long as possible. If a person does finally see the light, it can be disorienting and scary. That's why it's so important to lead people through the process, helping them to adjust to a brilliant new world.

Questions
- **What things keep people spiritually blind?**
  Read aloud Isaiah 35:3-5.
- **How can you minister to a spiritually blind person?**
- **Why can't people immediately see clearly after being blind?**
- **Who is spiritually blind in your life, and how can you help them gain sight?**

Spiritual Disciplines | WAX ON, WAX OFF

Humor

Title: THE KARATE KID (PG)
Columbia Pictures, 1984

Scripture: 1 Corinthians 9:24-27

Alternate Takes: Mentoring (Philippians 4:8-9),
Dedication (Revelation 3:15-16)

Themes R-Z

START TIME:	53 minutes, 45 seconds
START CUE:	Mr. Miyagi comes out.
END TIME:	56 minutes, 30 seconds
END CUE:	Mr. Miyagi walks back inside at night.
DURATION:	2 minutes, 45 seconds

Overview: Mr. Miyagi tells Daniel that he must dedicate himself fully to karate because he can't merely dabble in it. To learn, Daniel will have to follow without question everything Mr. Miyagi says. Daniel agrees, and Mr. Miyagi sets him to work waxing his cars.

Illustration: People who wish to follow in the footsteps of Jesus must dedicate themselves fully to the task. The spiritual disciplines provide one way to grow and prepare for discipleship. Challenge your students to make the disciplines, such as fasting, prayer, and silence, part of their spiritual training to grow strong and mature in their faith.

Questions

• **Can a person become an expert at something without continually practicing? Why or why not?**

Read aloud 1 Corinthians 9:24-27.

• **What activities should Christians practice continually in order to become excellent disciples?**

• **What is the goal of practicing spiritual disciplines?**

• **What is one discipline you want to begin practicing, and how will you make it a lasting habit?**

Spiritual Heritage | I'M ROYALTY?!

Title: THE PRINCESS DIARIES (G)
Walt Disney Productions, 2001

Scripture: Galatians 3:23-29

Alternate Takes: Responsibility (Matthew 5:13-16), King Josiah (2 Kings 22:1-13)

START TIME:	13 minutes, 00 seconds
START CUE:	Mia stirs her tea.
END TIME:	15 minutes, 45 seconds
END CUE:	Mia runs away.
DURATION:	2 minutes, 45 seconds

Overview: Queen Renaldi reveals to Mia that her father was the Prince of Genovia and that she is a princess, the only heir to the throne. Mia can't believe it, since she planned to be invisible to the world.

Illustration: Sometimes God's kids forget that they're royalty. Use this scene to reaffirm participants' spiritual lineage and to challenge them to take up their crowns, living lives worthy of their heavenly Father.

Questions

- **What would you do if you became a king or queen?**
- **What rights are given to the child or legal heir of a king?**
  Read aloud Galatians 3:23-29.
- **What responsibilities do we have as an heir of God's kingdom?**
- **How can you honor your spiritual heritage this week?**

Spiritual Warfare | CALLING ALL OSTRICHES

Title: PEARL HARBOR (PG-13)
Touchstone Pictures, 2001

Scripture: Ephesians 6:10-13

Alternate Takes: Sin of Omission (James 4:17), Defense (Genesis 14:8-20)

START TIME:	Tape/Disc 1, 32 minutes, 30 seconds
START CUE:	Screen shows exterior of the White House.
END TIME:	Tape/Disc 1, 33 minutes, 30 seconds
END CUE:	President Roosevelt says, "…while our enemies build bombs."
DURATION:	1 minute

Overview: President Roosevelt wonders how long America is going to pretend the world isn't at war. Europe needs the U.S. military, but U.S. citizens think Hitler's not their problem.

Illustration: Many Christians pretend spiritual warfare is someone else's problem—such as missionaries, Christians in India, or exorcists! Discuss this clip to wake up participants to the fact that the entire world is at war spiritually and they need to join in the fight now.

Questions

- **Do you believe in spiritual warfare? Why or why not?**
- **How does Satan make himself evident in our society and in the world?**
  Read aloud Ephesians 6:10-13.
- **What makes preparing for battle so important for Christians?**
- **How can you prepare yourself for spiritual warfare?**

Stewardship | IS THIS A SMART BUY?

Title: FATHER OF THE BRIDE (PG)
Touchstone Pictures, 1991

Scripture: Deuteronomy 8:17-18

Alternate Takes: "Christianese" (1 Corinthians 14:8-11),
Put-Downs (Proverbs 11:12)

START TIME:	41 minutes, 45 seconds
START CUE:	Franck enters.
END TIME:	44 minutes, 30 seconds
END CUE:	Franck claps and leaves.
DURATION:	2 minutes, 45 seconds

Overview: Franck goes over the wedding plans. George can't understand a word of Franck's mangled English and nearly loses consciousness when he learns the wedding cake costs twelve hundred dollars.

Illustration: We have a responsibility to create spending habits that glorify God. Give your young people a righteous framework for making their purchases as they strive to become God-honoring financial stewards.

Questions

- What is the most ridiculous waste of money you've ever heard of?
- What motivates a person to spend their money frivolously?
  Read aloud Deuteronomy 8:17-18.
- Can you glorify God when spending money on yourself? Explain.
- How could you become a better steward of your money? Be specific.

Strength | I CAN RUN FOREVER!

Title: CHARIOTS OF FIRE (PG)
Warner Bros., 1981

Scripture: Isaiah 40:26-31

Alternate Take: Victory (Deuteronomy 20:1-4)

START TIME:	1 hour, 34 minutes, 15 seconds
START CUE:	People enter church.
END TIME:	1 hour, 36 minutes, 30 seconds
END CUE:	A man sits on a bench in defeat.
DURATION:	2 minutes, 15 seconds

Overview: Eric Liddell preaches from Isaiah 40 while the Olympic event he was supposed to compete in is held across town. He speaks of God giving men strength to overcome obstacles while we simultaneously see men fall in defeat on the racetrack.

Illustration: It's hard to find strength in a world that seems to beat us down at every turn. That's why God promises to grant strength to all who turn their eyes upon him.

Questions

- **When do you feel weak, both physically and spiritually?**
  Read aloud Isaiah 40:26-31.
- **How does God give strength to his children?**
- **What can prevent people from turning to God when they feel weak or fall down?**
- **Where do you need strength most in your life right now, and how can you turn that area over to God?**

Stress | I'M GONNA BLOW!!

Title: BEST IN SHOW (PG-13)
Warner Bros., 2000

Scripture: Psalm 94:16-19

Alternate Take: Kindness (Galatians 5:22-25)

START TIME:	57 minutes, 45 seconds
START CUE:	Meg enters a pet store.
END TIME:	59 minutes, 00 seconds
END CUE:	Meg exits.
DURATION:	1 minute, 15 seconds

Overview: Meg frantically searches for a stuffed bear in a bumblebee costume at a pet store. She can't find exactly what she's looking for and freaks out.

Illustration: While this situation is ridiculous, Meg's reaction is common. We see people snapping under stress in public more and more each day. Use this discussion to help teenagers turn toward the peace of Christ in times of stress, showing them how to cope with crisis constructively.

Questions

- **When was the last time you were stressed out? What happened?**
- **How do you usually deal with stress?**
  Read aloud Psalm 94:16-19.
- **How can you calm your anxious thoughts?**
- **What are the root causes of stress in your life, and how can you turn them over to God?**

Title: THE PRINCE OF EGYPT (PG)
DreamWorks SKG, 1998

Scripture: Jeremiah 7:22-24

Alternate Takes: Pride (2 Samuel 22:26-28),
Pharaoh (Exodus 8:16-19)

START TIME:	1 hour, 10 minutes, 30 seconds
START CUE:	Rameses asks, "Why can't things be the way they were before?"
END TIME:	1 hour, 12 minutes, 15 seconds
END CUE:	Moses says, "Rameses, you bring this upon yourself."
DURATION:	1 minute, 45 seconds

Overview: Rameses blames everything on Moses. Moses counters that Rameses' stubbornness provoked the plagues. Something worse will happen unless he releases Israel. Rameses won't listen, promising to deal harshly with the Hebrews.

Illustration: No one wants to mirror Rameses' stubbornness. Use this clip to help teenagers find a balance between standing up for themselves and bringing disaster upon themselves because of stubborn pride.

Questions

- **Why are stubborn people so tough to deal with?**
- **What motivates a person's stubbornness?**
  Read aloud Jeremiah 7:22-24.
- **How can you keep your heart soft and free of stubbornness?**
- **What are some methods for dealing with stubborn people?**

Submission | **NO BOW!**

Title: CROUCHING TIGER, HIDDEN DRAGON (PG-13)
Sony Pictures Classics, 2000

Scripture: Ephesians 5:19-21

Alternate Takes: Mentoring (Titus 2:1-8),
Discipleship (Matthew 4:18-20)

START TIME:	43 minutes, 15 seconds
START CUE:	Mu Bai exits the shadows.
END TIME:	46 minutes, 15 seconds
END CUE:	Yu flies away.
DURATION:	3 minutes

Overview: Mu Bai offers to train Yu. He can help her control and use the knowledge she has. Yu refuses, unwilling to place herself under the power of another.

Illustration: *Submission* sounds like profanity these days. Redeem this word by explaining God's view of submission and how it actually helps a person grow.

Questions

- What comes to your mind when you hear the word *submit*?
- Why does society typically attach a negative connotation to the word *submit*?

  Read aloud Ephesians 5:19-21.

- Why does God want us to submit to others?
- Should you ever refuse to submit to someone? If so, when?
- What areas of your life do you need to submit to others, and how can you do that?

Suicide | GOODBYE

Title: DEAD POETS SOCIETY (PG)
Touchstone Pictures, 1989

Scripture: Ecclesiastes 2:17-20

Alternate Takes: Depression (Psalm 42), Tragedy (Job 5:1-8)

START TIME:	1 hour, 44 minutes, 15 seconds
START CUE:	The doorknob turns.
END TIME:	1 hour, 45 minutes, 45 seconds
END CUE:	Neil sits at the desk staring at a gun.
DURATION:	1 minute, 30 seconds

Overview: Neil walks downstairs and gets his father's pistol out of the desk, preparing to kill himself.

Illustration: Suicide never provides the correct answer. Help your students deal with their depression by turning to God when life seems hopeless.

Questions

- Why might a person see suicide as the answer to problems?
  Read aloud Ecclesiastes 2:17-20.
- Why did Solomon feel so hopeless? Can you relate? Why or why not?
- How can a person deal with suicidal feelings?
- How can you help someone who's dealing with suicide or with suicidal feelings?

Talents | SHOW ME YOURS

Title: MISS CONGENIALITY (PG-13)
Warner Bros., 2000

Scripture: Matthew 25:14-30
Alternate Takes: Self-Image (Psalm 139:13-16),
The Body (1 Corinthians 12:22-31)

START TIME:	51 minutes, 30 seconds
START CUE:	The Miss USA talent competition begins.
END TIME:	53 minutes, 15 seconds
END CUE:	Gracie rings bells as part of her performance.
DURATION:	1 minute, 45 seconds

Overview: The Miss USA contestants show off their various talents—singing, dancing, twirling—and Gracie caps it off with a wacky song and dance.

Illustration: It doesn't matter what your talent is, whether it's accounting, synchronized swimming, or telling jokes, God wants us to do all things for his glory. Discuss this scene as a way to encourage your youth to let their talents point to God by shining before others.

Questions
- **What are your talents?**
- **Are some talents more important than others? Explain.**
  Read aloud Matthew 25:14-30.
- **Why doesn't God give everyone the same number of talents?**
- **How can your talents be used to glorify God?**

Thought Life | AT LEAST THEY CAN'T HEAR ME

Title: WHAT WOMEN WANT (PG-13)
Paramount Pictures, 2000

Scripture: 2 Corinthians 10:5-7
Alternate Takes: God's Omniscience (1 Chronicles 28:9),
Compassion (1 John 3:17-18)

START TIME:	35 minutes, 45 seconds
START CUE:	Nick says, "Here's what happened."
END TIME:	37 minutes, 00 seconds
END CUE:	Morgan asks, "What girl with the fruit?"
DURATION:	1 minute, 15 seconds

Overview: Nick explains that he can hear exactly what every woman thinks. Morgan doesn't believe him. Nick notices the depressed thoughts of a girl in his office.

Illustration: A completely different world might be going on inside of our heads than what others see. God doesn't just want righteous actions, though; he asks for a mind and thought life turned toward the stuff of heaven. Use this clip to suggest ways we can gain control of our thoughts and glorify God with both our bodies and our brains.

Questions

- **What would happen if people could hear your thoughts?**
  Read aloud 2 Corinthians 10:5-7.
- **What makes our thought life as important as our physical actions?**
- **How can a person learn to capture his or her thoughts for God?**
- **What are some thought patterns you need to change, and how can you do that?**

Time | SPARE A MINUTE?

Title: LARA CROFT: TOMB RAIDER (PG-13)
Paramount Pictures, 2001

Scripture: Psalm 90:10-17

Alternate Take: Sorrow (Genesis 49:33–50:2)

START TIME:	1 hour, 6 minutes, 30 seconds
START CUE:	"I know what you want, Lara."
END TIME:	1 hour, 7 minutes, 45 seconds
END CUE:	Lara exits.
DURATION:	1 minute, 15 seconds

Overview: Manfred Powell tells Lara that the triangle gives the possessor the power of God to move back and forth in time and make things right. With it she could regain the time she lost with her father.

Illustration: Time is the world's most precious commodity. No matter how hard we try, we can't save, bend, or stretch it. That's why it's so important to use time wisely. Discover ways to make the most of time and discern where to place it.

Questions

- **What would you do if you could control time?**
- **Why is our society so obsessed with time management?**
  Read aloud Psalm 90:10-17.
- **Do you agree with this perspective on time? Why or why not?**
- **How can you make better use of your time this week?**

Title: MEET THE PARENTS (PG-13)
Universal Pictures, 2000

Scripture: Proverbs 3:5-8
Alternate Take: Omniscience (Job 34:21-22)

START TIME:	16 minutes, 00 seconds
START CUE:	Jack says, "Let me ask you a question, Greg."
END TIME:	17 minutes, 15 seconds
END CUE:	Jack says, "We'll be watching you."
DURATION:	1 minute, 15 seconds

Overview: Jack shows Greg and Pam his "baby-sitter cam"—hidden motion-activated cameras. Greg believes you can trust other people, but Jack strongly disagrees. He explains that's why he's always watching people wherever they go in the house.

Illustration: With government cover-ups, backstabbing friends, abusive parents, and scandals involving clergy, it's hard to know who to trust these days. God truly is trustworthy and promises to lead his children on the path to righteousness. Use this discussion to explore why trust seems like an endangered species and what it takes to become trustworthy in a world filled with suspicion.

Questions
- **What prevents people from trusting each other?**
- **What does it take to earn your trust?**
  Read aloud Proverbs 3:5-8.
- **How has God proven himself trustworthy in your life?**
- **How can you become a trustworthy person to others?**

Title: A CIVIL ACTION (PG-13)
Touchstone Pictures, 1998

Scripture: Psalm 43
Alternate Takes: Justice (Romans 2:1-3),
Lawsuits (1 Corinthians 6:1-6)

START TIME:	1 hour, 12 minutes, 45 seconds
START CUE:	Jerry sits down.
END TIME:	1 hour, 15 minutes, 00 seconds
END CUE:	Jerry stands.
DURATION:	2 minutes, 15 seconds

Overview: Jerry tells Jan he's never waited for a jury before. He hypothesizes that he'll get off because verdicts always come down to people—people who are easily persuaded. Jan responds that the jury members will see the truth. Jerry scoffs, "The courtroom isn't a place to look for truth."

Illustration: The truth is out there, but so many people either look for it in the wrong places or deny it even exists. Point to the only real source of truth, God's Word, and show ways that its ancient unchanging truth gives the ultimate guidance for life.

Questions

- **Why can't people agree on what truth is?**
- **Where do people look for their source of truth?**
  Read aloud Psalm 43.
- **What makes God the ultimate source of truth?**
- **How can God's truth help you overcome trials in the future?**

Unconditional Love | NOTHING TAKES IT AWAY

Title: A.I.: ARTIFICIAL INTELLIGENCE (PG-13)
Warner Bros., 2001

Scripture: Psalm 136
Alternate Take: Loving God (Joshua 22:5)

Start Time:	4 minutes, 45 seconds
Start Cue:	Sheila's face closes.
End Time:	6 minutes, 45 seconds
End Cue:	Professor Hobby says, "Didn't God create Adam to love him?"
Duration:	2 minutes

Overview: Sheila gives a physiological description of what love is. Professor Hobby wants a robot that will love unconditionally. A woman asks if they can get a human to love the robot back. Hobby claims their robot will be perfect and always loving. The woman persists, asking what responsibility a person has toward a robot that loves him or her.

Illustration: Unconditional love is hard to find and even harder to grasp. God dispenses it freely to us, though, whether we accept it or not. Define unconditional love, where it can be found, and what responsibility we have to the God who loves us so completely and perfectly.

Questions

- **What images come to mind when you think about unconditional love?**
  Read aloud Psalm 136.

- Has God proven to you that his love endures forever? If so, how?
- What are some ways God has shown his love to the world? to you personally?
- What responsibility do you have toward the God who loves you unconditionally?

Unity | WE'RE IN THE ARMY NOW

Title: INDEPENDENCE DAY (PG-13)
20th Century Fox, 1996

Scripture: Colossians 3:9-15

Alternate Take: Freedom From Sin (Romans 6:11-14)

START TIME:	1 hour, 47 minutes, 15 seconds
START CUE:	The president grabs the microphone.
END TIME:	1 hour, 49 minutes, 00 seconds
END CUE:	The crowd cheers.
DURATION:	1 minute, 45 seconds

Overview: The president inspires the troops with a speech. They're about to be part of the largest aerial battle in the history of mankind. They can't be consumed by petty differences because the world is united to fight for freedom and the right to live. They're fighting for independence!

Illustration: Christians around the world should be joining arm in arm to fight against the real enemy who is striving to destroy the world—Satan. Unfortunately, many Christians spend their time bickering with one another. Encourage teenagers to look for opportunities to reach across denominational lines and fight side by side with other Christians for the kingdom of God.

Questions
- **Who is the common enemy of every follower of Christ?**
- **What boundaries keep Christians of different denominations from joining together in a spiritual army?**
  Read aloud Colossians 3:9-15.
- **What would happen if Christians truly lived by these verses?**
- **How can we break down some of the barriers that exist between Christians from different denominations or different backgrounds?**

Violence | I DIDN'T SEE IT COMING

Title: AS GOOD AS IT GETS (PG-13)
   TriStar Pictures, 1997

Scripture: Isaiah 59:1-9
Alternate Takes: Evil (Matthew 15:17-20), Tragedy (Job 21)

START TIME:	24 minutes, 45 seconds
START CUE:	Simon says, "Want some water?"
END TIME:	25 minutes, 45 seconds
END CUE:	Verdell, the dog, barks.
DURATION:	1 minute, 00 seconds

Overview: Simon discovers people robbing his house. He asks simply, "Why are you doing this?" The thieves viciously beat him in response.

Illustration: Violence is becoming more common on our streets and within schools. Use this compelling scene to talk about violence, its origin in the human heart, and how a Christian can respond to this explosive problem.

Questions
   • **Why do we glorify violence in the media and video games?**
   • **How have you seen violence in the news or in your life recently?**
   Read aloud Isaiah 59:1-9.
   • **Where does violence come from?**
   • **How can Christians minister to the victims of violence or to violent people?**

War | WHAT'S IT GOOD FOR?

Title: THE FIFTH ELEMENT (PG-13)
   Columbia Pictures, 1997

Scripture: Psalm 46
Alternate Takes: Hope (Psalm 25:1-3), Evil (Genesis 4:1-9)

START TIME:	1 hour, 51 minutes, 15 seconds
START CUE:	Leeloo chooses "W" on the computer.
END TIME:	1 hour, 52 minutes, 00 seconds
END CUE:	Leeloo trembles with fear.
DURATION:	45 seconds

Overview: Leeloo watches images of war flash across the computer screen.

Illustration: Humanity can't seem to leave war behind. God allows for times of war, but it isn't always easy for Christians to discern when and where war is appropriate. Seek God's heart and mind on the subject, giving those involved in your ministry a biblical perspective on humanity's ravaging pastime.

Questions

- **What wars are going on around the world right now?**
- **Why do people still go to war, knowing the horrible consequences?**
  Read aloud Psalm 46.
- **Why doesn't God stop war on earth?**
- **Is it ever necessary to go to war? Why or why not? How do you decide?**
- **What is a Christian's responsibility during times of war?**

The World | DON'T TOUCH ME!

Title: BUBBLE BOY (PG-13)
Touchstone Pictures, 2001

Scripture: Matthew 5:13-16
Alternate Take: Purity (Job 14:1-4)

START TIME:	30 seconds
START CUE:	A nurse rolls a baby down a hall.
END TIME:	2 minutes, 45 seconds
END CUE:	Mom uses an *icthus* cookie cutter on dough.
DURATION:	2 minutes, 15 seconds

Overview: The bubble boy's home is outfitted with protective bubbles and tubes. His mom promises to keep him completely protected from the world.

Illustration: Many Christians try to become "bubble people" by totally disconnecting from the world. While we shouldn't indulge in sinful desires, God does call us to infect the world as salt and light. Use this silly scene to challenge participants to live in and change the world, without becoming like it.

Questions

- **Why do Christians sometimes try to completely avoid the world?**
- **Is it possible to protect yourself that way? Why or why not?**
  Read aloud Matthew 5:13-16.
- **How will the world receive light if Christians separate themselves from the world?**
- **How can you spread salt and light without getting infected by the world's vices?**

Title: THE MUMMY (PG-13)
Universal Pictures, 1999

Scripture: John 14:6

Alternate Takes: Fear (Psalm 23), Faith (Judges 10:11-16)

START TIME:	1 hour, 6 minutes, 45 seconds
START CUE:	The Mummy traps Beni.
END TIME:	1 hour, 8 minutes, 15 seconds
END CUE:	The Mummy asks, "Where are the other sacred jars?"
DURATION:	1 minute, 30 seconds

Overview: Beni pulls out several necklaces with a different religious symbol hanging from each one (Jewish, Buddhist, Muslim, Christian, and so on) to ward off the Mummy. Beni calls upon each religion's god to save him.

Illustration: People pick, choose, borrow, and steal from every religion under the sun to create a worldview that works for them, making Christ's claim as the one-way ticket to heaven sound somewhat rigid when compared to a universalist approach. Use this clip to talk about world religions, how they relate to one another and to Christianity, and why Jesus is the only way to the Father.

Questions

- **What elements of other religions do you find appealing? Why?**
- **What are some things other religions believe that seem completely crazy to you?**

  Read aloud John 14:6.

- **Is it fair to people who devote themselves to other religions for Jesus to be the only way to God? Why or why not?**
- **What things make Christianity unique when compared to other world religions?**
- **How can you talk with people from other faiths about Christianity without getting into an argument?**

Themes R-Z

MOVIE BACKGROUND INDEX

A.I.: Artificial Intelligence (PG-13) Warner Bros., 2001...10, 135
A robotic boy named David (Haley Joel Osment) embarks on a quest for the Blue Fairie who will transform him into a real boy who "deserves" the unconditional love of the mother that abandoned him.

As Good As It Gets (PG-13) TriStar Pictures, 1997...28, 69, 137
Obsessive-compulsive Melvin's (Jack Nicholson) orderly life gets disrupted by the assault on his gay neighbor Simon (Greg Kinnear) and his growing love for working-class waitress Carol (Helen Hunt).

At First Sight (PG-13) MGM, 1999...125
Amy (Mira Sorvino) falls for a hunky blind masseuse named Virgil (Val Kilmer), encouraging him to undergo surgery that will restore his vision.

Bandits (PG-13) MGM, 2001...51
Joe (Bruce Willis) and Terry (Billy Bob Thornton) break out of prison, sweep across the country, rob banks, and fall in love with Kate (Cate Blanchett), a depressed housewife who joins their escapades.

Batman (PG-13) Warner Bros., 1989...48, 57
Billionaire Bruce Wayne (Michael Keaton) dons the garb of Batman, ridding Gotham City of its criminals. Things get sticky for the caped crusader with the appearance of the devious Joker (Jack Nicholson) and the lovely reporter Vicki Vale (Kim Basinger).

Bedazzled (PG-13) 20th Century Fox, 2000...31, 37
Lovable loser Elliot (Brendan Fraser) makes a deal with the devil (Elizabeth Hurley) to trade his soul for seven wishes that will help him win the heart of Alison (Frances O'Connor).

Behind Enemy Lines (PG-13) 20th Century Fox, 2001...98
Chris Burnett (Owen Wilson) gets shot down behind enemy lines in Bosnia and must run for his life until Admiral Reigart (Gene Hackman) can rescue him.

Movie Background Index

Best in Show (PG-13) Warner Bros., 2000...30, 123, 129

This "mockumentary" follows the misadventures of various wacky dog owners who compete in the Mayflower Kennel Club Dog Show.

Big (PG) 20th Century Fox, 1988...32, 104

Twelve-year-old Josh receives his wish to become big, waking up one morning in the body of an adult (Tom Hanks).

Bring It On (PG-13) Universal Pictures, 2000...89

Cheerleading captain Torr Shipman (Kirsten Dunst) leads her squad to the national competition, hoping to defeat the rival Clovers from Compton.

Brokedown Palace (PG-13) 20th Century Fox, 1999...15

Alice (Claire Danes) and Darlene (Kate Beckinsdale) get imprisoned in Thailand when police discover illegal drugs in their bags.

Bubble Boy (PG-13) Touchstone Pictures, 2001...138

Jimmy Livingston (Jake Gyllenhaal) spends his entire life encased in a plastic bubble due to his faulty immune system. When his true love Chloe decides to marry a jerk, he suits up on a cross-country trip to stop her.

Can't Buy Me Love (PG-13) Touchstone Pictures, 1987...24, 35

Ultra-geek Ronald Miller (Patrick Dempsey) pays the school's most popular girl, Cindy Mancini (Amanda Peterson), to go out with him for a month in order to help him become popular.

Cast Away (PG-13) 20th Century Fox, 2000...52, 65, 69

Chuck Noland (Tom Hanks) finds himself stranded on a remote island, forced to fight against the elements in order to survive.

Chariots of Fire (PG) Warner Bros., 1981...111, 128

This movie is based on the true story of two determined sprinters, Eric Liddell (Ian Charleson), a Christian, and Harold Abrahams (Ben Cross), a Jew, who compete in the 1924 Olympics.

Charlie's Angels (PG-13) Columbia Pictures, 2000...39

Natalie (Cameron Diaz), Dylan (Drew Barrymore), and Alex (Lucy Liu) form the detective trio hired to discover who wants to steal Eric Knox's cellphone voice-tracking software.

Chicken Run (G) DreamWorks SKG, 2000...25

Ginger (Julia Sawalha) desperately wants to escape the Tweedy chicken farm with all of her friends and believes she's found the answer with the unexpected arrival of Rocky (Mel Gibson), a chicken who can fly!

A Christmas Story (PG) MGM, 1983...61, 100
Ralph's only dream is to receive a Red Rider BB gun on Christmas day, but hilarious fate and a wacky family seem bent on preventing it.

The Cider House Rules (PG-13) Miramax Films, 1999...22
Homer (Tobey Maguire) leaves the orphanage he grew up in to find himself out in the "real world," working on an apple farm and falling in love with Candy (Charlize Theron).

A Civil Action (PG-13) Touchstone Pictures, 1998...67, 134
Slick personal injury lawyer Jan Schlichtmann (John Travolta) takes up the cause of a small town whose citizens experience terrible sickness and death due to the waste dumped into the river by different companies.

Crouching Tiger, Hidden Dragon (PG-13) Sony Pictures Classics, 2000...130
Master Li Mu Bai (Chow Yun-Fat) and Yu Shu Lien (Michelle Yeoh) try to recover the magical Green Destiny sword from a rebellious and incredibly talented swordswoman, Jen Yu (Ziyi Zhang).

Dead Poets Society (PG) Touchstone Pictures, 1989...33, 79, 93, 131
Passionate English professor John Keating (Robin Williams) inspires his students at an uptight prep school to *carpe diem*—take risks and enjoy life to the fullest.

Disney's The Kid (PG) Walt Disney Productions, 2000...100
Heartless consultant Russell Duritz (Bruce Willis) learns the importance of enjoying life when he meets himself as an eight-year-old kid.

Dr. Dolittle 2 (PG) 20th Century Fox, 2001...43
Dr. Dolittle (Eddie Murphy) must convince two endangered bears to mate in order to save the forest from being stripped.

Dr. Suess' How the Grinch Stole Christmas (PG)
Universal Pictures, 2000...22, 92, 114
This is a live action version of the classic tale of the miserly Grinch (Jim Carrey) who hates Christmas and all who celebrate it.

The Emperor's New Groove (G) Walt Disney Productions, 2000...117
Self-absorbed Emperor Kuzco (David Spade) learns the importance of helping others when he's turned into a llama.

E.T. the Extra-Terrestrial (PG) Universal Pictures, 1982...42, 101

Elliot discovers a lost alien living in his back yard and helps him escape the government agents trying to capture him on his journey "home."

Father of the Bride (PG) Touchstone Pictures, 1991...86, 128

George Banks (Steve Martin) grapples with the bittersweet emotions (and neurosis) of seeing his baby girl get married.

Field of Dreams (PG) Universal Pictures, 1989...113

Farmer Ray Kinsella (Kevin Costner) hears a voice calling him to plow under his crop and build a baseball field, guaranteeing "he will come."

The Fifth Element (PG-13) Columbia Pictures, 1997...16, 96, 137

Korben Dallas (Bruce Willis) helps Leeloo (Milla Jovovich) recover the stones that will save the universe from destruction by an alien force.

Finding Forrester (PG-13) Columbia Pictures, 2000...10

Reclusive novelist William Forrester (Sean Connery) takes on talented writer and basketball player Jamal Wallace (Rob Brown) as his apprentice.

Hardball (PG-13) Paramount Pictures, 2001...71

Gambler and all around loser Conor O'Neill (Keanu Reeves) takes over an inner-city little league team and learns the importance of being there for others.

Home Alone (PG) 20th Century Fox, 1990...49, 105, 111

Kevin (Macaulay Culkin) gets left behind over the Christmas holidays and must defend his house from two bumbling burglars.

Hoop Dreams (PG-13) Fine Line Features, 1994...75, 80, 107

This documentary follows the divergent paths of two promising high school basketball players over the course of four years.

The House of Mirth (PG) Sony Pictures Classics, 2000...60

Beautiful socialite Lily Bart (Gillian Anderson) tries to find a wealthy husband who will support her but risks missing out on true love.

The Hudsucker Proxy (PG) Warner Bros., 1994...76, 87

Evil corporate raider Sidney Mussburger (Paul Newman) tries to manipulate wide-eyed optimist Norville Barnes (Tim Robbins) into ruining Hudsucker Industries so he can cash in on the stock.

In & Out (PG-13) Paramount Pictures, 1997...120
An ex-student wins an Academy Award and thanks his small town "gay" teacher Howard Brackett (Kevin Kline)...who's scheduled to get married.

Independence Day (PG-13) 20th Century Fox, 1996...122, 136
Aliens invade earth, and it's up to several brave Americans to fight back and save the human race.

Indiana Jones and the Temple of Doom (PG) Paramount Pictures, 1984...84
Indiana Jones (Harrison Ford) must free thousands of child slaves from the clutches of an evil pagan priest who rules the Temple of Doom.

The Iron Giant (PG) Warner Bros., 1999...112
A boy befriends a giant robot and tries to hide him from the government.

Jurassic Park (PG-13) Universal Pictures, 1993...21, 32
A living amusement park filled with resurrected dinosaurs goes horribly wrong as the "entertainment" starts eating all of the guests.

Jurassic Park III (PG-13) Universal Pictures, 2001...46
Dr. Alan Grant (Sam Neill) returns to Jurassic Park to try and rescue a lost boy.

The Karate Kid (PG) Columbia Pictures, 1984...125
New kid in town Daniel (Ralph Macchio) learns lessons about karate and life from enigmatic handyman and martial arts master Mr. Miyagi (Pat Morita).

Keeping the Faith (PG-13) Touchstone Pictures, 2000...36, 47
Childhood friends Jake (Ben Stiller) and Brian (Edward Norton) become a rabbi and priest respectively and both fall in love with Anna Riley (Jenna Elfman).

A Knight's Tale (PG-13) Columbia Pictures, 2001...23
Commoner William (Heath Ledger) defies tradition and enters jousting competitions to prove he's worthy of the title *knight* and the hand of beautiful Jocelyn (Shannyn Sossamon).

Lara Croft: Tomb Raider (PG-13) Paramount Pictures, 2001...133
Adventurer Lara Croft (Angelina Jolie) must find the two missing pieces of an ancient talisman in order to prevent the Illuminati from controlling time.

A League of Their Own (PG) Columbia Pictures, 1992...73, 119

Sisters Dottie (Geena Davis) and Kit (Lori Petty) leave home to join manager Jimmy Dugan (Tom Hanks) and play in the All-American Girls Professional Baseball League during World War II.

Left Behind: The Movie (PG) Cloud Ten, 2001...76

Chaos reigns as the Rapture hits, taking the faithful away and forcing those "left behind" to turn to God or the antichrist.

Legally Blonde (PG-13) MGM, 2001...18, 43

Sorority queen Elle Woods (Reese Witherspoon) heads to Harvard Law School in order to win back the heart of her ex-boyfriend Warner (Matthew Davis) and decides to prove everyone wrong by becoming a lawyer while she's at it.

The Lord of the Rings: The Fellowship of the Ring (PG-13) New Line Cinema, 2001...11, 44

Humble hobbit Frodo Baggins (Elijah Wood) must carry a magical evil into the depths of Mordor and destroy it before Sauron (Sala Baker) covers Middle-earth with darkness.

The Majestic (PG) Warner Bros., 2001...12, 77

Blacklisted screenwriter Pete (Jim Carrey) crashes his car and gets amnesia. The small town of Lawson mistakes him for lost war hero Luke and welcomes him with open arms...until the truth comes out.

The Man in the Moon (PG-13) MGM, 1991...52

Fourteen-year-old Dani (Reese Witherspoon) quickly comes of age when she falls in love with seventeen-year-old Court (Jason London)...who develops a passionate relationship with Dani's older sister, Maureen (Emily Warfield).

Meet the Parents (PG-13) Universal Pictures, 2000...39, 64, 134

Greg (Ben Stiller) endures the worst weekend of his life, trying to win the approval of his overbearing prospective father-in-law Jack (Robert DeNiro) despite his ever-increasing blunders.

Men in Black (PG-13) Columbia Pictures, 1997...14, 25

The super secret Men in Black patrol all of the alien life on earth. Agent K (Tommy Lee Jones) trains his new partner J (Will Smith) while trying to prevent a cockroach alien from destroying the world.

The Mighty (PG-13) Miramax Films, 1998...38, 41

This movie depicts the heartwarming friendship between Kevin, a physically disabled brainiac, and Max, a powerful dimwit, who become greater when they join together.

Miss Congeniality (PG-13) Warner Bros., 2000...132
FBI agent Gracie Hart (Sandra Bullock) goes undercover as a beauty contestant in order to foil the bombing of a pageant.

Mission: Impossible (PG-13) Paramount Pictures, 1996...17
Secret agent Ethan Hunt (Tom Cruise) must steal top secret information so he can prove his innocence.

Mission: Impossible II (PG-13) Paramount Pictures, 2000...49
Ethan Hunt (Tom Cruise) convinces beautiful thief Nyah (Thandie Newton) to return to her cutthroat boyfriend Sean (Dougray Scott) so that he and Nyah can discover the location of a deadly virus Sean stole.

Moulin Rouge! (PG-13) 20th Century Fox, 2001...81, 87
Penniless writer Christian (Ewan McGregor) and beautiful courtesan Satine (Nicole Kidman) fall in love while staging an elaborate play, but discover many obstacles standing in the way of their happiness.

The Mummy (PG-13) Universal Pictures, 1999...139
Adventurer Rick O'Connell (Brendan Fraser) must protect Evie (Rachel Weisz) and Jonathan after accidentally awakening evil sorcerer Imhotep (Arnold Vosloo) from his imprisonment.

The Mummy Returns (PG-13) Universal Pictures, 2001...108
Rick (Brendan Fraser) and Evie O'Connell (Rachel Wiesz) fight for the life of their son when Imhotep is reawakened.

My Dog Skip (PG) Warner Bros., 2000...13, 91
Willie (Frankie Muniz) comes of age in 1940s Mississippi through his relationship with his dog, Skip.

Mystery Men (PG-13) Universal Pictures, 1999...115, 117
A ragtag band of misfit pseudo-superheroes must protect Champion City from Casanova Frankenstein (Geoffrey Rush) after he captures Captain Amazing (Greg Kinnear).

The Naked Gun: From the Files of Police Squad! (PG-13) Paramount Pictures, 1988...94, 110
Bumbling Los Angeles police detective Drebin (Leslie Nielsen) attempts to foil a plot to assassinate the queen of England.

O Brother, Where Art Thou? (PG-13)
Touchstone Pictures, 2000...82, 97, 102, 123
Everett (George Clooney), Pete (John Turturro), and Delmar (Tim Blake Nelson) bust out of jail in the Depression-era South and hightail it across the country to rescue Everett's buried treasure, and to stop his wife from marrying someone else.

Ocean's Eleven (PG-13) Warner Bros., 2001...95
Danny Ocean (George Clooney) leads a band of thieves in their impossible plan to rob three Las Vegas casinos at once.

Orange County (PG-13) Paramount Pictures, 2002...66, 92
Shaun (Colin Hanks) longs to attend Stanford, but everything and everyone in his life seems to be conspiring to keep him stuck in Orange County.

The Others (PG-13) Dimension Films, 2001...36
Grace (Nicole Kidman) and her photosensitive children live trapped inside a house they fear has been invaded by ghosts.

Pay It Forward (PG-13) Warner Bros., 2000...53, 66, 73
Trevor (Haley Joel Osment) devises a simple plan to change the world: Help someone else and then challenge him or her to help three others.

Pearl Harbor (PG-13) Touchstone Pictures, 2001...34, 83, 127
A love triangle between two best friends (Ben Affleck and Josh Hartnett) and the nurse they love (Kate Beckinsale) explodes on the date that shall forever be remembered in infamy.

The Perfect Storm (PG-13) Warner Bros., 2000...120
This movie is based on the true story of the fishing boat Andrea Gail that got caught in the middle of the ocean during one of the most punishing storms in history.

Planet of the Apes (PG-13) 20th Century Fox, 2001...89
Stranded astronaut Leo Davidson (Mark Wahlberg) must escape from a planet populated by apes who enslave humans.

The Prince of Egypt (PG) DreamWorks SKG, 1998...84, 88, 90, 130
This movie is an animated retelling of the story of Moses and the exodus of the Jewish people from Egypt.

The Princess Diaries (G) Walt Disney Productions, 2001...126
Mia (Anne Hathaway) discovers she is actually a princess and must undergo intense lessons with Queen Renaldi (Julie Andrews) before she can be presented as royalty.

Rat Race (PG-13) Paramount Pictures, 2001...27, 54

Nine people receive keys to a locker in Silver City, New Mexico, that contains two million dollars. The first person to get there wins the money.

Remember the Titans (PG) Walt Disney Productions, 2000...16, 68, 105

This movie is based on the true story of the T.C. Williams High School football team who, forced to racially integrate, went to the state championship under the leadership of its black coach, Herman Boone (Denzel Washington).

Return to Me (PG) MGM, 2000...55

Widowed contractor Bob (David Duchovny) falls in love with Grace (Minnie Driver), who is the transplant recipient of Bob's deceased wife's heart.

Riding in Cars With Boys (PG-13) Columbia Pictures, 2001...108, 118

Based on the true story of Beverly D'Onofrio (Drew Barrymore), this movie depicts Beverly's struggle to overcome the adversity of a teenage pregnancy to follow her dream of becoming an author.

Rocky (PG) United Artists, 1976...116

Working-class boxer Rocky Balboa (Sylvester Stallone) gets the shot of a lifetime to square off in the ring against heavyweight champion Apollo Creed (Carl Weathers).

Rush Hour (PG-13) New Line Cinema, 1998...99

Fast-talking LAPD detective James Carter (Chris Tucker) joins martial arts guru Chinese detective inspector Lee (Jackie Chan) on his quest to rescue the kidnapped daughter of a diplomat.

Rush Hour 2 (PG-13) New Line Cinema, 2001...70

Carter (Chris Tucker) and Lee (Jackie Chan) re-team to take down an elaborate international counterfeiting ring.

Save the Last Dance (PG-13) Paramount Pictures, 2001...61

Through the love of African-American Derek (Sean Patrick Thomas), white girl Sara (Julia Stiles) copes with adjusting to inner-city life after the death of her mother.

Shanghai Noon (PG-13) Touchstone Pictures, 2000...59

Imperial Guard Chon Wang (Jackie Chan) travels to the wild West and joins fast-talking cowboy Roy O'Bannon (Owen Wilson) to save kidnapped Princess Pei Pei (Lucy Liu).

Shrek (PG) DreamWorks SKG, 2001...13, 26, 46
Uncouth ogre Shrek (Mike Myers) and Donkey (Eddie Murphy) rescue Princess Fiona (Cameron Diaz) from a dragon so she can marry jerk Lord Farquaad.

Sister Act (PG) Touchstone Pictures, 1992...50, 62, 96
Vegas lounge singer Deloris (Whoopi Goldberg) must flee the mob by hiding in a convent as a nun.

The 6th Day (PG-13) Columbia Pictures, 2000...113
Adam Gibson (Arnold Schwarzenegger) fights to get his life back from the clone who stole it and the evil multibillionaire Drucker who funded the cloning project.

Smoke Signals (PG-13) Miramax Films, 1998...121
Tough guy Victor and utter nerd Thomas join an uneasy alliance as they leave the reservation to retrieve the belongings of Victor's deadbeat dad.

The Spitfire Grill (PG-13) Columbia Pictures, 1996...59, 74
Percy, an ex-con, arrives in the small town of Gillead hoping to make a new life for herself.

Star Trek V: The Final Frontier (PG) Paramount Pictures, 1989...55
The crew of the Enterprise journeys to the center of the universe to meet God.

Stargate (PG-13) MGM, 1994...58
Egyptologist Daniel Jackson (James Spader) and special forces Colonel O'Neil (Kurt Russell) journey through the Stargate to another world ruled by a despotic leader who wants to enslave the earth.

Superman (PG) Warner Bros., 1978...20, 102, 103
Clark Kent (Christopher Reeve) uses his super powers to keep the peace and stop Lex Luthor's (Gene Hackman) diabolical plan to detonate nuclear bombs along the San Andreas fault.

Tomorrow Never Dies (PG-13) MGM, 1997...124
British secret agent 007, James Bond (Pierce Brosnan), must foil a media mogul's plot to create news by instigating World War III.

Twister (PG-13) Warner Bros., 1996...29, 85, 106
Storm chasers Bill (Bill Paxton) and Jo (Helen Hunt) battle the fiercest tornado system in history while trying to repair their broken marriage.

U-571 (PG-13) Universal Pictures, 2000...40
This movie is based on the true story of the daring mission to capture a German enigma coding machine from a submarine and use it to decode transmissions.

Unbreakable (PG-13) Touchstone Pictures, 2000...109
David Dunn (Bruce Willis) becomes the only survivor of a catastrophic train wreck, leading him to believe he might possibly have super powers.

A Walk to Remember (PG) Warner Bros., 2002...19, 72
High school bad boy Landon gets a lesson about life and the true meaning of love from resident "saint" Jamie (Mandy Moore).

What Lies Beneath (PG-13) DreamWorks SKG, 2000...63
Frazzled housewife Claire (Michelle Pfeiffer) believes she's seeing ghosts, while her husband Dr. Spencer (Harrison Ford) believes she's going crazy.

What Women Want (PG-13) Paramount Pictures, 2000...79, 132
Male chauvinist Nick (Mel Gibson) can suddenly hear all the thoughts of women and learns what they really want.

Where the Heart Is (PG-13) 20th Century Fox, 2000...78
Novalee Nation (Natalie Portman) carves a life for herself in the town of Sequoyah, Oklahoma after she's abandoned in a Wal-Mart to give birth to her child alone.

While You Were Sleeping (PG) Hollywood Pictures, 1995...64
Lucy (Sandra Bullock) saves businessman Peter (Peter Gallagher) and gets mistaken for his fiancée by the family, while falling in love with Peter's brother, Jack (Bill Pullman).

The Winslow Boy (G) Sony Pictures Classics, 1999...29
Arthur Winslow uses all of his family's resources to prove the innocence of his son who was accused of stealing a stamp.

X-Men (PG-13) 20th Century Fox, 2000...45, 56
The X-Men, an elite force of mutants with special powers, must stop Magneto's plan to turn the entire human race into mutants.

Zoolander (PG-13) Paramount Pictures, 2001...19, 81
Supermodel Derek Zoolander (Ben Stiller) must foil a plot to assassinate the prime minister of Malaysia.

SCRIPTURE INDEX

Scripture Index

TOPICAL INDEX